Building Microservices with Node.js: A Complete Guide for Developers

A Step-by-Step Guide to Scalable App Development with Node.js

BOOZMAN RICHARD

BOOKER BLUNT

Table of Content

TABLE OF CONTENTS

INTRODUCTION

Building Microservices with Node.js: A Complete Guide for Developers

The world of software development has undergone a significant transformation with the advent of **microservices architecture**. This architectural style has become the standard approach for building modern, scalable, and resilient applications. Microservices enable developers to break down complex systems into smaller, more manageable services, each focusing on a specific business capability. This modular approach allows for improved scalability, flexibility, and faster deployment cycles, making it ideal for high-demand applications that require frequent updates, high availability, and fault tolerance.

Node.js, with its event-driven, non-blocking I/O model, is the perfect platform to build microservices. It is lightweight, efficient, and well-suited for handling the high concurrency that microservices often demand. Its vast ecosystem, driven by the **npm** package manager, provides developers with a wealth of tools and libraries to build everything from RESTful APIs to real-time communication systems. Node.js excels at building fast, efficient, and scalable services, making it a top choice for microservices architectures.

This book is designed as a comprehensive guide for developers who want to leverage **Node.js** to build and manage microservices. Whether you're a seasoned developer looking to migrate a monolithic application to microservices or a newcomer eager to explore the world of microservices, this book will provide you with the knowledge and practical skills to succeed.

What You Will Learn

The journey through this book will equip you with the skills to design, implement, and deploy Node.js microservices that are scalable, reliable, and easy to maintain. We begin by introducing you to the core concepts of microservices, including the benefits, challenges, and architectural principles that guide this approach. From there, we dive deep into the practical aspects of building microservices with Node.js, focusing on how to create independent, loosely-coupled services that can scale with demand and perform efficiently.

You'll learn how to:

- **Design Microservices**: Understand the principles and patterns behind microservice architectures, including communication protocols (e.g., REST, gRPC), data management strategies, and how to structure services for maximum scalability and reliability.

- **Build RESTful APIs**: Create APIs using Node.js and the Express framework, focusing on best practices for service communication, error handling, and security.

- **Manage Distributed Transactions**: Explore patterns like Saga and Two-Phase Commit (2PC) to handle transactions across multiple services, ensuring data consistency in a distributed environment.

- **Monitor and Maintain Services**: Learn the tools and techniques for monitoring the health of your services, managing configuration and secrets, and setting up alerting systems to catch issues before they escalate.

- **Test Microservices**: Master the strategies for unit testing, integration testing, and load testing microservices to ensure they perform well under high traffic and are resilient to failure.

- **Deploy and Scale**: Discover how to deploy your microservices to cloud platforms such as AWS, Azure, and Google Cloud, set up CI/CD pipelines for automated testing and deployment, and scale services based on demand.

Why Microservices and Node.js?

Microservices are more than just a trend—they are a paradigm shift in how we build software. Traditional monolithic applications, while simple at first, can become increasingly difficult to maintain and scale as the system grows. With microservices, each part of an application is independent, making it easier to update, scale, and even replace individual services without affecting the entire system.

Node.js fits naturally into the microservices world due to its lightweight, asynchronous nature, and ability to handle a large number of simultaneous requests with minimal overhead. This makes it ideal for applications that need to scale and handle real-time data. Furthermore, Node.js's non-blocking I/O model allows services to remain responsive even under high load, while its single-threaded event loop ensures that resources are used efficiently.

The Structure of the Book

This book is divided into 24 chapters, each focusing on a specific aspect of building microservices with Node.js. Here's a breakdown of what you can expect:

1. **Introduction to Microservices Architecture**: Learn the foundational principles of microservices and how they differ from monolithic applications.

2. **Setting Up Your Development Environment**: A step-by-step guide to getting Node.js and essential tools installed and configured.

3. **Building Your First Node.js Microservice**: Dive into creating a simple microservice, including routing, controllers, and error handling.

4. **Distributed Transactions and Consistency**: Explore techniques for ensuring data consistency in

a distributed environment, including the Saga Pattern and Two-Phase Commit (2PC).

5. **Service Communication**: Learn how services communicate with each other using RESTful APIs, message queues, and gRPC.

6. **Securing Microservices**: Discover how to secure your microservices, implement authentication and authorization, and ensure safe communication.

7. **Testing Microservices**: Learn how to write unit tests, integration tests, and performance tests for microservices to ensure reliability.

8. **Deploying and Scaling Microservices**: Master deploying your microservices to cloud platforms like AWS, Azure, and Google Cloud, and learn how to scale them based on demand.

9. **Monitoring and Maintenance**: Set up monitoring, logging, and alerting systems to keep your microservices healthy in production.

10. **Best Practices and the Future of Node.js Microservices**: Learn the best practices for building microservices that are maintainable, resilient, and scalable, and explore emerging trends and technologies in the Node.js ecosystem.

Who This Book Is For

This book is for developers, architects, and technical leads who are interested in mastering **Node.js** to build microservices. It's suitable for:

- **Beginner Node.js developers** looking to understand how to build microservices with Node.js.
- **Experienced backend developers** who want to move from monolithic systems to microservices architectures.
- **Tech leads and architects** who want to design scalable and resilient microservices-based systems.
- **DevOps engineers** who are responsible for deploying, monitoring, and maintaining microservices.

Why This Book Is Different

While there are many resources available on microservices, few focus specifically on building microservices with **Node.js**—a language that excels at building scalable and efficient microservices. This book is packed with **real-world examples** and hands-on exercises, allowing you to apply what you've learned directly to building production-ready microservices. Each chapter provides practical code snippets, architecture diagrams, and step-by-step explanations to ensure that you not only understand the theory behind microservices but also how to implement them in a real-world Node.js application.

By the end of this book, you'll be well-equipped to build, deploy, and maintain microservices using **Node.js**, ensuring that your applications are scalable, resilient, and efficient.

Conclusion

In today's fast-moving development world, microservices have become an essential architectural style for building modern applications. **Node.js**, with its performance and scalability, is the ideal platform for building these microservices. This book is your complete guide to mastering Node.js microservices—from the basic principles to advanced techniques, and from building resilient services to deploying them in the cloud.

Are you ready to take your Node.js development skills to the next level and embrace the world of microservices? Let's dive in and start building!

CHAPTER 1

INTRODUCTION TO MICROSERVICES ARCHITECTURE

What are Microservices?

Microservices refer to a software architectural style where a large application is broken down into smaller, independently deployable services, each responsible for a specific business function. Each service operates as a standalone unit, with its own database, and communicates with other services through well-defined APIs. This contrasts with a monolithic architecture, where all components are tightly integrated into a single application.

Microservices are often used in large-scale applications because they allow teams to work on individual services independently, scale specific parts of the system, and deploy features without affecting the entire application.

Benefits of Microservices

1. **Scalability**: Since microservices are independent, you can scale each service individually depending on the load. For example, a service handling user authentication can

be scaled more easily than other parts of the application that do not experience high traffic.

2. **Resilience**: A failure in one service does not necessarily affect the entire system. Each microservice is isolated, so issues in one service can be managed and resolved without causing downtime in others.

3. **Flexibility in Technology Choices**: Different microservices can be written in different programming languages, using different databases or technologies. This provides the flexibility to choose the best tools for each individual service.

4. **Faster Time to Market**: Microservices allow teams to develop, test, and deploy individual services independently, accelerating the development cycle and reducing time to market for new features.

5. **Improved Fault Isolation**: Because services are decoupled, they can handle failures better. Even if one service fails, the rest of the application continues to function.

Challenges of Microservices

1. **Complexity**: While microservices help to break down a large application, they introduce complexity in terms of managing multiple services. Each service needs to be individually monitored, logged, and maintained.

17

2. **Data Management**: Managing data consistency across distributed services can be difficult, especially when it involves transactions that span multiple services. It's important to design the system to handle eventual consistency.

3. **Network Latency**: Communication between services typically happens over the network, which can introduce latency. This may affect the performance of the application, especially when services need to communicate frequently.

4. **Deployment and Monitoring**: With multiple services running, it becomes necessary to implement efficient deployment pipelines and robust monitoring systems. Managing these distributed systems requires specialized tools and strategies.

5. **Increased Overhead**: Each service might need its own deployment pipeline, continuous integration, and other overheads associated with running individual microservices. This can increase operational costs and complexity.

Why Use Node.js for Microservices?

Node.js is an excellent choice for building microservices for several reasons:

1. **Non-Blocking I/O**: Node.js is built around asynchronous, non-blocking I/O, which makes it highly efficient for handling multiple concurrent requests. This is particularly useful in microservices architectures, where numerous services might need to handle high volumes of requests simultaneously.

2. **Scalability**: Node.js's event-driven model allows microservices to scale efficiently without adding much overhead. Node.js also works well with distributed systems, which is essential for microservices that need to communicate with each other.

3. **Lightweight and Fast**: Node.js is lightweight and provides quick response times, making it suitable for microservices that need to process requests quickly.

4. **Large Ecosystem**: Node.js has a rich ecosystem of libraries and frameworks (such as Express.js, Koa.js) that facilitate the development of microservices. The npm (Node Package Manager) registry provides a vast range of packages, speeding up development.

5. **Cross-Platform**: Node.js can run on various platforms, which makes it easy to deploy microservices in different environments such as on-premise servers, cloud infrastructure, or containerized environments like Docker.

6. **JSON for Communication**: Node.js works seamlessly with JSON, a common format for communication

between microservices. Since microservices often exchange data via HTTP APIs (like RESTful APIs), JSON is widely used for data serialization and deserialization, and Node.js handles it efficiently.

7. **Active Community and Support**: Node.js has an active developer community, which means ample resources, tutorials, and tools to support building microservices.

Real-World Example: Breaking Down a Monolithic App into Microservices

Consider a typical monolithic e-commerce application that handles various aspects such as product management, user authentication, order processing, payment processing, and inventory management. In a monolithic architecture, all these components are tightly coupled, meaning that a change in one module may require redeploying the entire application, making scaling and maintenance difficult.

Step 1: Identify Core Business Domains
The first step in breaking down a monolithic app into microservices is identifying distinct business domains. For example, an e-commerce application might break down into the following microservices:

- **Product Service**: Manages product listings, descriptions, and categories.

- **User Service**: Handles user authentication, registration, and profiles.
- **Order Service**: Manages customer orders, including order creation, updates, and status tracking.
- **Payment Service**: Processes payments and integrates with external payment gateways.
- **Inventory Service**: Tracks product stock levels and manages restocking.

Step 2: Decouple Services

Each service will be developed, deployed, and maintained independently. The services can communicate with each other using RESTful APIs or messaging systems (like RabbitMQ or Kafka). This decoupling allows the teams working on different services to work independently and avoid bottlenecks.

Step 3: Migrate Data

In the monolithic architecture, a single database often handles all data. In a microservices architecture, each service has its own database, which may require data migration and restructuring. For instance, the User Service might use a relational database (SQL), while the Product Service might use a NoSQL database (like MongoDB).

Step 4: Deployment and Scalability

Once the services are decoupled, they are deployed as individual units. Each service can be scaled independently based on demand.

For instance, during high traffic, the Product Service may need to be scaled more than the Inventory Service, which is less likely to experience the same load.

By using Node.js for these microservices, the e-commerce platform benefits from its lightweight nature, scalability, and fast performance.

Conclusion

Microservices allow for more flexibility, scalability, and resilience, especially when using technologies like Node.js. While the architecture introduces complexities, it significantly improves the maintainability and agility of applications, especially as they grow.

CHAPTER 2

SETTING UP YOUR DEVELOPMENT ENVIRONMENT

Installing Node.js and Necessary Tools

Before you can start building microservices with Node.js, it's essential to set up your development environment correctly. Here's how to get started:

1. **Install** **Node.js**

    Node.js is the runtime environment for executing JavaScript code outside the browser. To get started, you need to download and install Node.js.

    o **Visit the official Node.js website**: Go to https://nodejs.org/ and download the latest stable version (LTS).

    o **Installation**: The installation process is straightforward. Run the installer and follow the on-screen instructions.

    o **Verify Installation**: After installation, open your terminal or command prompt and type:

    ```bash
    node -v
    ```

This command will display the installed version of Node.js. You should see something like v16.0.0 (or whichever version is the latest LTS).

o **Verify npm (Node Package Manager)**: npm comes bundled with Node.js. To check if npm is installed, type:

bash

npm -v

This will display the version of npm installed.

2. **Install Additional Tools**

o **Git**: Git is a version control system that allows you to manage your code repositories. If you don't already have Git installed, you can download it from https://git-scm.com/.

o **Postman**: Postman is an essential tool for testing APIs. You can download it from https://www.postman.com/downloads/.

Introduction to Package Managers (npm, yarn)

Node.js projects often require external libraries or packages to be used for various purposes, such as connecting to a database or handling HTTP requests. These packages are managed by package managers.

1. **npm (Node Package Manager)**

   npm is the default package manager for Node.js. It allows you to install, manage, and share code libraries. With npm, you can install both local and global packages.

   o **Local Installation**: Install packages specific to a project (e.g., Express for creating web servers).

   ```bash
   npm install express
   ```

   This installs the package in the `node_modules` directory and updates the `package.json` file.

   o **Global Installation**: Install packages globally for use in any project.

   ```bash
   npm install -g nodemon
   ```

   `nodemon` is useful for auto-restarting your server when file changes occur during development.

2. **Yarn**

   Yarn is an alternative package manager that aims to be

faster and more secure than npm. It offers features such as offline caching, faster installs, and deterministic dependency resolution.

    o   To install Yarn, you can use npm:

```bash
```

```bash
npm install -g yarn
```

    o   Once installed, you can use Yarn to manage packages:

```bash
```

```bash
yarn add express
```

Setting Up a Code Editor and Environment

A proper code editor is crucial for efficient development. Here's how to set up your development environment:

1. **Install Visual Studio Code (VSCode)** Visual Studio Code is one of the most popular and feature-rich code editors for web development. You can download it from https://code.visualstudio.com/.

    o   **Recommended Extensions for Node.js**:

          ▪   **ESLint**: Linting JavaScript code to catch errors early.

- **Prettier**: Code formatting tool for keeping your code clean and readable.
- **Node.js**: Adds Node.js support for debugging and running scripts.

2. **Configuring VSCode**
   - **Install the extensions** by going to the Extensions view (Ctrl+Shift+X) and searching for the recommended extensions.
   - **Set up a terminal inside VSCode**: You can open the terminal in VSCode by going to **View > Terminal** or using the shortcut (Ctrl+`).
   - **Use Git inside VSCode**: VSCode comes with built-in Git support, so you can manage your source control directly from the editor.

3. **Additional Tools**:
   - **Docker**: If you plan to use Docker for containerization, you can install the Docker Desktop application. It allows you to manage containers and images easily.
   - **MongoDB or PostgreSQL**: If your microservices require a database, install the necessary database systems (e.g., MongoDB or PostgreSQL) and configure them.

First Steps: Your First Microservice Project Setup

Now that your environment is set up, let's create your first microservice.

1. **Create a New Project Directory**
   Start by creating a new folder for your project. You can do this from the terminal:

   ```bash
   ```

   ```bash
   mkdir my-first-microservice
   cd my-first-microservice
   ```

2. **Initialize the Project**
   Use npm to initialize your project, which will generate a `package.json` file to manage your dependencies.

   ```bash
   ```

   ```bash
   npm init -y
   ```

3. **Install Necessary Packages**
   For the basic structure of your microservice, you will need Express.js, a lightweight framework for building web applications in Node.js:

   ```bash
   ```

28

```
npm install express
```

4. **Create the Server File**

   In your project directory, create a file named `server.js`. This file will handle incoming HTTP requests.

   Example of a basic server setup:

   ```javascript
   const express = require('express');
   const app = express();
   const port = 3000;

   app.get('/', (req, res) => {
     res.send('Hello, World!');
   });

   app.listen(port, () => {
     console.log(`Server running at http://localhost:${port}`);
   });
   ```

5. **Run the Server**

   Now, run the server with the following command:

   ```bash
   node server.js
   ```

29

If everything is set up correctly, your server should be running at `http://localhost:3000`, and visiting this URL in a browser will display "Hello, World!".

6. **Test**   **the**   **Endpoint**

Open Postman or a browser and test the endpoint by navigating to `http://localhost:3000/`. You should receive a "Hello, World!" message.

Conclusion

In this chapter, you've set up your development environment by installing Node.js, learning how to use package managers like npm and yarn, and configuring Visual Studio Code. You also started your first Node.js microservice project by setting up a basic server using Express. With this foundation, you're ready to dive deeper into developing and managing microservices with Node.js.

CHAPTER 3

UNDERSTANDING THE CORE CONCEPTS OF NODE.JS

Node.js is built on several core concepts that make it ideal for building scalable and efficient applications. In this chapter, we will explore these key concepts in depth and provide practical examples to help you understand how they work.

Event-Driven Architecture in Node.js

Node.js operates on an **event-driven architecture**, which means that the application doesn't wait for tasks to complete before moving on to the next one. Instead, it listens for events and responds to them when they occur. This model allows Node.js to handle many operations concurrently without blocking the main thread.

- **Event Loop**: At the heart of Node.js's event-driven model is the event loop. The event loop is responsible for executing all JavaScript code, collecting and processing events, and executing queued sub-tasks. It runs in a single thread and is non-blocking, meaning it can perform other tasks while waiting for I/O operations (like reading files,

31

making network requests, or querying a database) to complete.

- **How It Works**: When Node.js receives an I/O request, such as reading a file or making an HTTP request, it doesn't wait for the request to complete. Instead, it registers a callback function (an event listener) and moves on to process other tasks. Once the I/O operation completes, Node.js triggers the callback, thus handling the result asynchronously.

Real-world Example: Imagine you have an application that needs to read several files from the disk. In a traditional blocking approach, the application would wait for one file to finish reading before starting the next. But in Node.js, the event-driven model allows it to start reading multiple files at once, handling each file asynchronously as the operation completes, rather than waiting for each one to finish.

Non-Blocking I/O and Asynchronous Operations

A key feature of Node.js is its non-blocking I/O operations. Non-blocking means that Node.js can handle other requests while waiting for operations like reading from a file, making HTTP requests, or querying a database. This makes Node.js an excellent choice for applications that require high concurrency, such as web servers and real-time applications.

- **Blocking vs Non-Blocking I/O**:
  - **Blocking I/O**: In traditional programming languages like Java or Python, an I/O operation (e.g., reading a file) would block the execution of the program until the operation is complete. This means the program is paused while it waits for I/O operations to finish.
  - **Non-Blocking I/O**: In Node.js, I/O operations are non-blocking. When a request is made (e.g., to read a file), Node.js doesn't stop to wait for the request to complete. Instead, it continues executing other tasks, and once the file is read, a callback function is invoked to handle the result.
- **Example of Asynchronous Operation**: Here's how you might use non-blocking I/O with the `fs` (filesystem) module to read a file asynchronously:

```javascript
const fs = require('fs');

console.log('Start reading file');

fs.readFile('example.txt', 'utf8', (err, data) => {
  if (err) {
    console.error('Error reading file:', err);
```

```
  } else {
    console.log('File content:', data);
  }
});
```

```
console.log('File read initiated');
```

In this example, Node.js does not wait for the file to be read. The output will show:

```
arduino
```

```
Start reading file
File read initiated
File content: (contents of the file)
```

The `readFile` method is asynchronous, meaning Node.js can perform other tasks while waiting for the file to be read.

Introduction to Express.js: A Web Framework for Node.js

Express.js is a lightweight and fast web application framework built on top of Node.js. It simplifies the process of building web servers and APIs by providing easy-to-use tools for handling HTTP requests, routing, and middleware.

- **Why Use Express.js?**

- o **Simplicity**: Express provides a simple and clean API to handle HTTP requests, making it easier to manage routes, middleware, and error handling.
- o **Extensibility**: Express is highly extensible, meaning you can easily integrate other tools, middleware, or even build custom functionality.
- o **Community Support**: Express is one of the most popular web frameworks for Node.js, with a large and active community, which means plenty of resources, tutorials, and plugins.

- **Key Concepts of Express.js**:
  - o **Routes**: Routes define how the server should respond to various HTTP requests (GET, POST, PUT, DELETE) at specified URL paths.
  - o **Middleware**: Middleware functions are executed during the request-response cycle. They can modify the request object, the response object, or terminate the request-response cycle.
  - o **Request and Response**: Express provides a straightforward API for handling HTTP requests and sending responses.

Real-world Example: Setting Up a Basic Node.js Server with Express

Now that we understand the core concepts of Node.js, let's walk through setting up a basic web server using Express.js.

35

1. **Create a New Project Directory**
   Start by creating a new directory for your project and navigating into it:

   bash

   ```
   mkdir express-server
   cd express-server
   ```

2. **Initialize the Project**
   Initialize a new Node.js project with npm:

   bash

   ```
   npm init -y
   ```

3. **Install Express**
   Install Express using npm:

   bash

   ```
   npm install express
   ```

4. **Create the Server File**
   In the project directory, create a file called server.js. This will contain the basic server setup.

   javascript

```javascript
const express = require('express');
const app = express();
const port = 3000;

// Define a route for the home page
app.get('/', (req, res) => {
  res.send('Hello, World!');
});

// Start the server
app.listen(port, () => {
  console.log(`Server       running       at
http://localhost:${port}`);
});
```

In this code:

- o **express()**: Creates an Express application.
- o **app.get()**: Defines a route that handles GET requests to the home page (/).
- o **app.listen()**: Starts the server and listens on port 3000.

5. **Run   the   Server**

Run the server with the following command:

```bash
bash
```

```
node server.js
```

Your server should now be running, and you can visit `http://localhost:3000` in a browser. You should see the message "Hello, World!"

6. **Testing with Postman or Browser**
   You can use Postman or your browser to test the GET request to `http://localhost:3000`. You should receive the response `"Hello, World!"`.

Conclusion

In this chapter, we explored the core concepts of Node.js, including event-driven architecture, non-blocking I/O, and asynchronous operations, all of which make Node.js highly efficient for building scalable applications. We also introduced Express.js, a web framework that simplifies the creation of web servers and APIs in Node.js. Finally, we walked through setting up a basic server using Node.js and Express, giving you a solid foundation to start building your microservices. With this knowledge, you're ready to dive deeper into creating more complex microservices with Node.js.

CHAPTER 4

STRUCTURING YOUR MICROSERVICES

In this chapter, we will explore how to structure your microservices architecture and set up a Node.js project in a way that is scalable, maintainable, and easy to navigate. Structuring your microservices properly from the start is crucial for the long-term success of your application. We will also cover how to organize your code with services, controllers, and routes, which are essential components for building clean and efficient microservices.

Microservice Architecture Patterns

Microservices architecture is often organized into several distinct patterns that allow services to be loosely coupled while still being able to communicate with each other. Some common microservice architecture patterns include:

1. **Decomposition Patterns**:
   o **Domain-Driven Design (DDD)**: Decomposes the application into services based on business domains, such as users, orders, and payments.

39

This pattern is ideal when there are clear business boundaries.

o **Subdomain Decomposition**: A more granular approach, where microservices are split according to subdomains within a business domain (e.g., a "customer service" or "payment processing" service).

o **Functional Decomposition**: Splits services based on their functionality (e.g., a "product catalog" service and an "inventory" service).

2. **Communication Patterns**:

o **Synchronous Communication (REST APIs)**: Most microservices in modern web apps communicate synchronously over HTTP (RESTful APIs). This is the simplest form of communication but can lead to higher latency if there are many inter-service calls.

o **Asynchronous Communication (Message Queues)**: Some systems benefit from asynchronous messaging using tools like RabbitMQ or Kafka. Asynchronous messaging can help avoid bottlenecks and is useful in event-driven architectures.

3. **Data Management Patterns**:

o **Database Per Service**: Each microservice manages its own database, allowing the service to be autonomous. This pattern is recommended for scaling and resilience, but it can lead to challenges with data consistency across services.

o **Shared Database**: All services share a common database. This can simplify the architecture but may create dependencies and scalability issues, as changes to one service can affect others.

4. **API Gateway Pattern**:

o An API Gateway sits between the client and the microservices. It acts as a single entry point, routing requests to the appropriate microservice. It can also handle cross-cutting concerns like authentication, rate limiting, and logging.

How to Structure a Node.js Microservice Project

When structuring a Node.js microservice, the goal is to ensure that each microservice is independent, modular, and easy to scale. Here's a common directory structure for a Node.js microservice project:

bash

```
my-microservice/
|
├── src/
|    ├── controllers/          # Route handler
functions
```

41

```
|    ├─ services/          # Business logic and
data access
|    ├─ routes/            # API routes
definition
|    ├─ models/            # Database models
(e.g., MongoDB or Sequelize models)
|    ├─ middlewares/       # Middleware for
authentication, validation, etc.
|    ├─ config/            # Configuration files
(e.g., DB connection, environment variables)
|    └─ app.js             # Main entry point
for the application
|
├─ node_modules/           # Installed
dependencies (generated by npm)
├─ package.json            # Project metadata
and dependencies
└─ .env                    # Environment
variables (e.g., database credentials)
```

Explanation of Folders:

- **src/**: This is where all your application code resides. It's the core of your microservice.
  - **controllers/**: Contains functions that handle HTTP requests and responses. Controllers typically call the services layer to retrieve or modify data.

o **services/**: Encapsulates the business logic. Services often interact with databases, external APIs, or other microservices.

o **routes/**: Defines your HTTP routes (e.g., GET /users, POST /orders). Routes are connected to controllers to handle requests.

o **models/**: Defines database schemas and interacts with the database. For example, if you are using MongoDB, this would be where you define your Mongoose models.

o **middlewares/**: Contains functions that execute during the request-response cycle, such as authentication, logging, or input validation.

o **config/**: Houses all configuration files, like environment variables, database credentials, etc.

Organizing Your Code: Services, Controllers, and Routes

Now that we've discussed the overall structure, let's go deeper into how services, controllers, and routes are organized.

1. **Services**:

   o The **services** layer is responsible for handling business logic. It interacts with databases, APIs, and other external services.

   o For example, in a user service, the service could contain functions to create users, find users, and delete users, while the controller merely invokes these functions.

2. **Controllers**:

   o Controllers are responsible for handling HTTP requests and responses. They typically receive input from the client (e.g., query parameters, request body), pass it to the appropriate service, and return the results as a response.

   o For example, a `UserController` might handle creating a new user. It takes data from the request, calls the `UserService` to store the data, and returns a success or error message.

3. **Routes**:

   o Routes define how incoming requests are mapped to controllers. In Express.js, routes are often organized by functionality (e.g., user routes, order routes, etc.).

   o For example, a route for creating a new user might look like:

```javascript
const express = require('express');
const router = express.Router();
const         userController        =
require('../controllers/userControl
ler');
```

```
router.post('/users',
userController.createUser);
router.get('/users',
userController.getAllUsers);

module.exports = router;
```

4. **Middleware**:

   o Middleware functions allow you to add additional functionality to your request-response cycle. These are used for tasks like authentication, logging, validation, and error handling.

   o For example, a simple middleware to log incoming requests might look like:

   javascript

```
function logRequest(req, res, next)
{
   console.log(`${req.method}
${req.url}`);
   next(); // Pass control to the next
middleware
}
```

Real-world Example: Structuring a Simple E-commerce App

Let's take the example of a simple e-commerce app with the following services:

45

- **User Service**: Manages user accounts (registration, login).
- **Product Service**: Manages product listings (create, update, delete, retrieve).
- **Order Service**: Handles customer orders (create, track, cancel).

Here's how you would structure the code for the product service:

Folder structure:

```
graphql


product-service/
|
├── src/
|   ├── controllers/
|   |       └── productController.js      # Handles product-related requests
|   ├── services/
|   |       └── productService.js         # Contains business logic for products
|   ├── routes/
|   |       └── productRoutes.js          # Defines API routes for products
|   ├── models/
|   |       └── productModel.js           # Defines product schema for the database
```

```
|    └── app.js                    # Initializes
the server and connects everything
└── package.json                   # Project
metadata and dependencies
```

Product Service Example:

1. **Product Model (`productModel.js`)**:

    javascript

    ```javascript
    const mongoose = require('mongoose');

    const        productSchema      =        new
    mongoose.Schema({
      name: { type: String, required: true },
      price: { type: Number, required: true },
      description: String,
      category: String,
    });

    module.exports = mongoose.model('Product',
    productSchema);
    ```

2. **Product Service (`productService.js`)**:

    javascript

    ```javascript
    const              Product             =
    require('../models/productModel');
    ```

47

```
const createProduct = async (data) => {
  const product = new Product(data);
  await product.save();
  return product;
};

const getAllProducts = async () => {
  return await Product.find();
};

module.exports = {
  createProduct,
  getAllProducts,
};
```

3. **Product Controller (`productController.js`):**

```
javascript

const productService = require('../services/productService');

const createProduct = async (req, res) => {
  try {
    const product = await productService.createProduct(req.body);
    res.status(201).json(product);
  } catch (error) {
```

48

```
    res.status(500).json({          error:
error.message });
  }
};


const getAllProducts = async (req, res) =>
{
  try {
    const     products     =     await
productService.getAllProducts();
    res.status(200).json(products);
  } catch (error) {
    res.status(500).json({          error:
error.message });
  }
};


module.exports = {
  createProduct,
  getAllProducts,
};
```

4. **Product Routes (`productRoutes.js`)**:

```javascript
const express = require('express');
const router = express.Router();
```

```
const           productController           =
require('../controllers/productController
');

router.post('/products',
productController.createProduct);
router.get('/products',
productController.getAllProducts);

module.exports = router;
```

5. **App Setup (app.js):**

```
javascript

const express = require('express');
const mongoose = require('mongoose');
const           productRoutes           =
require('./routes/productRoutes');

const app = express();
app.use(express.json());

// Connect to MongoDB
mongoose.connect('mongodb://localhost/eco
mmerce',    {    useNewUrlParser:    true,
useUnifiedTopology: true });

// Use routes
app.use('/api', productRoutes);
```

```
const port = 3000;
app.listen(port, () => {
  console.log(`Product service running on
http://localhost:${port}`);
});
```

Conclusion

In this chapter, we covered how to structure a Node.js microservice project, using common patterns for organizing services, controllers, and routes. We also provided a real-world example of how to structure a product service in an e-commerce app. By organizing your microservices in a modular and maintainable way, you can scale your application more easily and ensure that it remains maintainable as it grows.

CHAPTER 5

DESIGNING YOUR FIRST MICROSERVICE

In this chapter, we will design and implement a basic microservice using Node.js. We will focus on creating an API, understanding RESTful APIs, and implementing CRUD (Create, Read, Update, Delete) operations. By the end of this chapter, you will have a solid foundation for designing and building your own microservices.

Designing the API for Your Microservice

When designing an API for a microservice, the goal is to ensure that the API is simple, clear, and easy to use for both developers and clients. The API should handle specific business functionalities in an isolated manner, meaning each microservice exposes only the necessary functionality required for other services or clients.

1. **Define Your Resources**: The first step in designing an API is identifying the resources your microservice will manage. For example, a user service might have resources such as "users" and "roles."

2. **Define**   **API**   **Endpoints**:
After identifying your resources, the next step is defining the endpoints for interacting with these resources. Each endpoint should correspond to a specific action you want to perform on a resource. Typically, RESTful APIs use standard HTTP methods (GET, POST, PUT, DELETE) to perform CRUD operations on resources.

Example endpoints for a **User Service**:

- **GET /users**: Retrieve all users.
- **GET /users/:id**: Retrieve a user by their unique ID.
- **POST /users**: Create a new user.
- **PUT /users/:id**: Update an existing user.
- **DELETE /users/:id**: Delete a user.

3. **Choose**   **a**   **Data**   **Format**:
RESTful APIs typically use JSON for data exchange between clients and services. JSON is lightweight, easy to parse, and widely supported by modern web clients.

Understanding RESTful APIs

A **RESTful API** is an architectural style for designing networked applications. It uses a stateless, client-server protocol to enable communication between systems. REST stands for

Representational State Transfer, and it emphasizes the following principles:

1. **Stateless**: Every request from the client to the server must contain all the information needed to understand and process the request (e.g., authentication, data). The server should not store any state about the client between requests.

2. **Uniform Interface**: The API should have a uniform and consistent interface. This includes using standard HTTP methods (GET, POST, PUT, DELETE) and conventions for resource naming (e.g., `/users`, `/products`).

3. **Client-Server Architecture**: The client and server are independent of each other, meaning the client is responsible for the user interface, and the server handles the data processing and business logic.

4. **Stateless Communication**: Each request from the client to the server must be self-contained. The server does not store the client's session or any previous request data.

5. **Representation of Resources**: Resources (such as users, products, etc.) are represented in a specific format, usually JSON or XML. Clients interact with resources by exchanging representations, typically via HTTP requests and responses.

6. **Cacheable**: Responses from the server should indicate whether the data can be cached to improve performance. This is particularly important for read-heavy APIs.

Implementing CRUD Operations in Node.js

In this section, we'll walk through how to implement the basic CRUD operations in Node.js for a user service. We will use **Express.js** for handling the HTTP routes and **MongoDB** (via the Mongoose library) for storing user data.

1. **Install** **Dependencies**

   First, let's install the required packages for our project:

   bash

   ```
   npm install express mongoose body-parser
   ```

2. **Set** **Up** **MongoDB** **Connection**

   We will connect to a local MongoDB database for storing user data.

   Create a file called db.js:

   javascript

   ```
   const mongoose = require('mongoose');

   mongoose.connect('mongodb://localhost/use
   rService', { useNewUrlParser: true,
   useUnifiedTopology: true })
     .then(() => console.log('Connected to
   MongoDB...'))
   ```

```
.catch(err => console.error('Could not
connect to MongoDB...', err));
```

3. **Define the User Model**

   We'll define the schema for the User resource, which will
   include the user's name and email.

   Create a file called userModel.js:

   javascript

```
const mongoose = require('mongoose');

const userSchema = new mongoose.Schema({
  name: { type: String, required: true },
  email: { type: String, required: true,
unique: true },
});

module.exports = mongoose.model('User',
userSchema);
```

4. **Create the User Service**

   Next, we'll create the service that interacts with the
   database. This service will have methods to create, read,
   update, and delete users.

   Create a file called userService.js:

```javascript
const User = require('./userModel');

const createUser = async (data) => {
  const user = new User(data);
  return await user.save();
};

const getAllUsers = async () => {
  return await User.find();
};

const getUserById = async (id) => {
  return await User.findById(id);
};

const updateUser = async (id, data) => {
  return await User.findByIdAndUpdate(id,
data, { new: true });
};

const deleteUser = async (id) => {
  return await User.findByIdAndDelete(id);
};

module.exports = {
  createUser,
  getAllUsers,
```

```
getUserById,
updateUser,
deleteUser
};
```

5. **Create the User Controller**

The controller will handle the incoming HTTP requests
and delegate the business logic to the user service.

Create a file called userController.js:

javascript

```
const userService =
require('./userService');

const createUser = async (req, res) => {
  try {
    const user = await
userService.createUser(req.body);
    res.status(201).json(user);
  } catch (err) {
    res.status(400).json({ message:
err.message });
  }
};

const getAllUsers = async (req, res) => {
  try {
```

```
    const      users      =        await
userService.getAllUsers();
    res.status(200).json(users);
  } catch (err) {
    res.status(400).json({         message:
err.message });
  }
};

const getUserById = async (req, res) => {
  try {
    const      user      =        await
userService.getUserById(req.params.id);
    if (!user) {
      return         res.status(404).json({
message: 'User not found' });
    }
    res.status(200).json(user);
  } catch (err) {
    res.status(400).json({         message:
err.message });
  }
};

const updateUser = async (req, res) => {
  try {
    const      user      =        await
userService.updateUser(req.params.id,
req.body);
```

```
    if (!user) {
        return        res.status(404).json({
message: 'User not found' });
    }
    res.status(200).json(user);
  } catch (err) {
    res.status(400).json({        message:
err.message });
  }
};

const deleteUser = async (req, res) => {
  try {
    const       user       =       await
userService.deleteUser(req.params.id);
    if (!user) {
        return        res.status(404).json({
message: 'User not found' });
    }
    res.status(200).json({ message: 'User
deleted successfully' });
  } catch (err) {
    res.status(400).json({        message:
err.message });
  }
};

module.exports = {
  createUser,
```

```
    getAllUsers,
    getUserById,
    updateUser,
    deleteUser
};
```

6. **Set**   **Up**   **Routes**

Now, we'll create the routes for the user API. These routes will map HTTP methods to controller functions.

Create a file called userRoutes.js:

javascript

```javascript
const express = require('express');
const router = express.Router();
const             userController            =
require('./userController');

router.post('/users',
userController.createUser);
router.get('/users',
userController.getAllUsers);
router.get('/users/:id',
userController.getUserById);
router.put('/users/:id',
userController.updateUser);
router.delete('/users/:id',
userController.deleteUser);
```

```
module.exports = router;
```

7. **Initialize the Express Server**
Finally, we will wire everything together in the app.js
file and start the server.

Create the app.js file:

```javascript

const express = require('express');
const mongoose = require('mongoose');
const bodyParser = require('body-parser');
const userRoutes = require('./userRoutes');

const app = express();
app.use(bodyParser.json());

mongoose.connect('mongodb://localhost/userService', { useNewUrlParser: true, useUnifiedTopology: true })
    .then(() => console.log('Connected to MongoDB...'))
    .catch(err => console.error('Could not connect to MongoDB...', err));

app.use('/api', userRoutes);
```

```
const port = 3000;
app.listen(port, () => {
  console.log(`User service running on
http://localhost:${port}`);
});
```

Conclusion

In this chapter, we designed the API for a user service, understanding how to define resources, endpoints, and the HTTP methods needed for a RESTful API. We then implemented the core CRUD operations in Node.js using Express.js and MongoDB. By following this approach, you can build microservices that handle specific business functions in a clean, maintainable way. With this foundation, you're ready to expand your knowledge and build more complex microservices.

CHAPTER 6

HANDLING REQUESTS AND RESPONSES IN NODE.JS

In this chapter, we will dive deeper into handling HTTP requests and responses in Node.js using the **Express.js** framework. Express simplifies the routing of requests and sending of responses. We will also explore the concept of **middleware** in Node.js, which allows us to handle requests before they reach the main logic. By the end of this chapter, you'll understand how to effectively manage requests and responses in a Node.js application, improving both functionality and maintainability.

Working with Express.js Routing

Routing in Express is a fundamental concept that helps you define how the server will respond to client requests. Each route is associated with a URL path and an HTTP method (e.g., GET, POST, PUT, DELETE). Express makes it easy to handle different routes and their associated logic.

Basic Routing Example:

```javascript
.
```

```
const express = require('express');
const app = express();

// Route handling a GET request to the homepage
app.get('/', (req, res) => {
  res.send('Welcome to the homepage!');
});

// Route handling a POST request
app.post('/submit', (req, res) => {
  res.send('Form submitted successfully');
});

const port = 3000;
app.listen(port, () => {
  console.log(`Server         running         at
http://localhost:${port}`);
});
```

In the example above:

- **GET** /: This route handles HTTP GET requests to the root path ("/").
- **POST /submit**: This route handles HTTP POST requests to "/submit".

Express supports routing for all HTTP methods and provides flexibility for defining path parameters, query parameters, and even wildcard routes.

Dynamic Routing Example (Path Parameters):

javascript

```javascript
app.get('/users/:id', (req, res) => {
  const userId = req.params.id;
  res.send(`User ID is ${userId}`);
});
```

In this example, :id is a **route parameter**. When a request is made to /users/123, the value 123 will be accessible via req.params.id.

Query Parameters:

javascript

```javascript
app.get('/search', (req, res) => {
  const query = req.query.q;   // Accessing the 'q' query parameter
  res.send(`You searched for: ${query}`);
});
```

For a request like /search?q=nodejs, the query parameter q will be accessed as req.query.q.

Sending Responses: Status Codes and Headers

When a request is made to the server, you need to send a response. Express provides an easy way to send responses, along with optional status codes and headers. The response can include:

- **Status Codes**: Indicates the outcome of the request.
- **Headers**: Metadata about the response, such as content type, caching policies, etc.
- **Body**: The actual data returned to the client.

Example of Sending Responses:

```javascript
app.get('/', (req, res) => {
  res.status(200).send('Request successful!');
});
```

- **res.status(200)**: Sets the HTTP status code to 200 (OK), indicating the request was successful.
- **res.send()**: Sends the response body as plain text.

Common HTTP Status Codes:

- **200 OK**: The request was successful, and the server returned the requested data.
- **201 Created**: The request was successful, and a new resource was created.

67

- **400 Bad Request**: The request was invalid (e.g., missing parameters).
- **404 Not Found**: The requested resource could not be found.
- **500 Internal Server Error**: An error occurred on the server.

Example with JSON Response:

javascript

```javascript
app.get('/user', (req, res) => {
  const user = { id: 1, name: 'Alice' };
  res.status(200).json(user);   // Respond with
JSON data
});
```

Sending Custom Headers:

javascript

```javascript
app.get('/headers', (req, res) => {
  res.set('Custom-Header', 'Value123');
  res.status(200).send('Custom header added');
});
```

In this example, a custom header Custom-Header is added to the response.

Middleware in Node.js: Handling Requests Before They Reach the Main Logic

Middleware is a powerful feature in Express.js that allows you to handle requests before they reach the actual route handler. Middleware functions are executed sequentially in the order they are defined. They can be used for a variety of tasks, such as authentication, logging, validation, and error handling.

Example of Middleware:

```javascript
const express = require('express');
const app = express();

// Middleware function to log request details
app.use((req, res, next) => {
  console.log(`${req.method} request made to ${req.url}`);
  next();  // Call the next middleware or route handler
});

// Route handler
app.get('/', (req, res) => {
  res.send('Hello, World!');
});
```

```
app.listen(3000, () => {
  console.log('Server is running on port 3000');
});
```

In this example, every incoming request triggers the middleware function, which logs the HTTP method and URL before passing control to the next middleware or route handler.

Middleware functions can also modify the request (req) or response (res) objects, or terminate the request-response cycle (for example, by sending a response directly).

Example of Using Middleware for Authentication:

javascript

```
const authenticate = (req, res, next) => {
  if (req.headers['authorization']) {
    next();   // If authorization header exists,
continue to the next handler
  } else {
    res.status(403).send('Forbidden:         No
authorization header');
  }
};


app.use(authenticate);   // Apply the middleware
to all routes
```

```
app.get('/protected', (req, res) => {
  res.send('This is a protected resource!');
});
```

Here, the `authenticate` middleware checks if the request contains an authorization header. If not, it sends a 403 (Forbidden) response; otherwise, it passes control to the next route handler.

Real-World Example: Implementing Validation Middleware

In many applications, validating incoming data is crucial to ensure that it meets specific criteria before the main logic processes it. For example, validating user input during user registration or form submissions.

Let's create a validation middleware for a user registration service that checks if the incoming request contains valid data.

1. **User Validation Middleware**:

```javascript
const validateUserData = (req, res, next) => {
  const { name, email, password } = req.body;

  // Check if all fields are provided
  if (!name || !email || !password) {
    return    res.status(400).json({    error:
'Missing required fields' });
```

71

```
}

// Check if email is valid
const emailRegex = /^[a-zA-Z0-9._-]+@[a-zA-Z0-
9.-]+\.[a-zA-Z]{2,4}$/;
if (!emailRegex.test(email)) {
    return      res.status(400).json({      error:
'Invalid email format' });
}


next();   // Proceed to the next middleware or
route handler
};
```

2. **Using the Validation Middleware**:

javascript

```
app.post('/register',   validateUserData,   (req,
res) => {
  const { name, email, password } = req.body;


  // Proceed with user registration logic (e.g.,
save to database)
  res.status(201).json({      message:      'User
registered successfully', user: { name, email }
});
});
```

Explanation:

- The `validateUserData` middleware checks if the request body contains the required fields (`name`, `email`, `password`).

- It also validates the email format using a regular expression.

- If any validation fails, it sends a 400 (Bad Request) response with an appropriate error message.

- If validation passes, it calls `next()` to pass control to the next handler, which in this case is the route handler for the user registration (`/register`).

Conclusion

In this chapter, we explored how to handle HTTP requests and responses in Node.js using Express.js. We covered how to create routes, send responses with status codes and headers, and implement middleware to process requests before they reach the main logic. Additionally, we walked through implementing validation middleware, a real-world use case that ensures data integrity before proceeding with business logic. By mastering these concepts, you can create robust and scalable APIs that handle a wide range of use cases.

CHAPTER 7

CONNECTING MICROSERVICES WITH RESTFUL APIS

In this chapter, we will explore how microservices communicate with each other. We'll focus on the two primary communication models: **synchronous** and **asynchronous** communication. Then, we'll dive into building RESTful APIs to facilitate these communications between services. Finally, we will implement a real-world example where an **Order Service** communicates with a **Payment Service** via RESTful APIs.

How Microservices Communicate: Synchronous vs Asynchronous Communication

Microservices often need to interact with each other to perform complex tasks. The communication between services can be categorized into two types:

1. **Synchronous Communication**:
   o In synchronous communication, one service makes a request to another and waits for the response before proceeding. This is the most common form of communication for client-server interactions and is often used in web applications.

- o **Example**: A customer places an order on an e-commerce website. The **Order Service** sends a request to the **Payment Service** to process the payment, and the **Order Service** waits for the payment response before confirming the order.

Advantages:

- o Simple to implement and understand.
- o Real-time communication between services.

Disadvantages:

- o Can lead to bottlenecks since each service is dependent on the response of the other.
- o If one service is slow or down, it can impact the entire system.

Use Cases:

- o When immediate feedback is required.
- o Payment processing, order confirmations, etc.

2. **Asynchronous Communication**:
   - o In asynchronous communication, services communicate without waiting for an immediate response. The calling service sends a request, and the called service processes it at its own pace. Once the processing is done, the result is

communicated back, often through a messaging queue or event-driven system.

- o **Example**: After an order is placed, the **Order Service** sends a message to a queue, which is then picked up by the **Payment Service** to process the payment. The **Order Service** does not wait for a response and can continue processing other orders.

Advantages:

- o No bottlenecks since services do not wait for each other's response.
- o Better fault tolerance; if a service is down, the message can be retried.

Disadvantages:

- o More complex to implement because it often requires additional infrastructure (message queues, event buses).
- o Responses are not instant, which can make it difficult to track the status of operations in real time.

Use Cases:

76

- o When services do not need an immediate response.
- o Email notifications, background tasks, data processing jobs, etc.

Building RESTful APIs for Communication

When building microservices, RESTful APIs are the most common method of communication. REST (Representational State Transfer) is an architectural style for distributed systems and is based on a stateless, client-server communication model.

Key Concepts of RESTful APIs:

- **Stateless**: Each request from a client to a server must contain all the necessary information to understand and process the request.
- **Client-Server**: The client and server are independent; the server handles the data, and the client handles the user interface.
- **Uniform Interface**: The API should be consistent and follow standard conventions like HTTP methods (GET, POST, PUT, DELETE).
- **Cacheable**: Responses must define whether they can be cached.

Creating a Simple RESTful API in Node.js (Express):

javascript

```
const express = require('express');
const app = express();
app.use(express.json());

// Example route for creating an order
app.post('/orders', (req, res) => {
  const orderData = req.body;
  // Logic to create an order
  res.status(201).send({ message: 'Order created
successfully', order: orderData });
});

// Example route for getting the status of an
order
app.get('/orders/:id', (req, res) => {
  const orderId = req.params.id;
  // Logic to get order by ID
  res.status(200).send({ message: `Order with
ID: ${orderId}`, status: 'Processing' });
});

const port = 3000;
app.listen(port, () => {
  console.log(`Order Service running on
http://localhost:${port}`);
});
```

In this example, we defined two RESTful endpoints:

1. **POST /orders**: Creates a new order.
2. **GET /orders/:id**: Fetches the status of an order by its ID.

These endpoints could be part of an Order Service, and the same approach can be used to implement other services (e.g., Payment Service, Product Service).

Real-World Example: Connecting an Order Service with a Payment Service

Let's now create a real-world example where an **Order Service** communicates with a **Payment Service** to handle payments for customer orders. We'll use synchronous communication (RESTful API calls) between the services.

Order Service

The Order Service will accept incoming orders and then call the Payment Service to process payments. If the payment is successful, the Order Service will confirm the order.

1. **Order Service Code**:

```javascript
const express = require('express');
```

```javascript
const axios = require('axios');  // To make HTTP
requests to the Payment Service
const app = express();
app.use(express.json());


// POST route to create an order
app.post('/orders', async (req, res) => {
  const { userId, amount } = req.body;

  try {
    // Step 1: Make an API request to Payment
Service to process the payment
    const        paymentResponse      =        await
axios.post('http://localhost:4000/payments', {
      userId,
      amount
    });

    if (paymentResponse.status === 200) {
      // Step 2: If payment is successful, create
the order
      res.status(201).send({   message:    'Order
created successfully', paymentStatus: 'Success'
});
    } else {
      res.status(400).send({   message:   'Payment
failed', paymentStatus: 'Failed' });
    }
  } catch (err) {
```

```javascript
    console.error('Error  processing  payment:',
err);
    res.status(500).send({    message:    'Error
processing payment' });
  }
});

const port = 3000;
app.listen(port, () => {
  console.log(`Order    Service    running    on
http://localhost:${port}`);
});
```

In this code, the Order Service sends an HTTP POST request to the Payment Service to process the payment. It waits for the response (synchronous communication) and proceeds based on whether the payment was successful or not.

Payment Service

The Payment Service will handle payment processing. For simplicity, let's assume the payment processing is just a simulated task.

2. **Payment Service Code:**

```javascript
javascript

const express = require('express');
```

```javascript
const app = express();
app.use(express.json());

// POST route to process payment
app.post('/payments', (req, res) => {
  const { userId, amount } = req.body;
  // Simulate payment processing logic
  console.log(`Processing payment for user
${userId} of amount $${amount}`);

  // Simulate successful payment
  if (amount > 0) {
    res.status(200).send({ message: 'Payment
processed successfully' });
  } else {
    res.status(400).send({ message: 'Payment
failed' });
  }
});

const port = 4000;
app.listen(port, () => {
  console.log(`Payment Service running on
http://localhost:${port}`);
});
```

In the Payment Service, when a POST request is received at
/payments, the service processes the payment and sends a
success or failure message back to the Order Service.

Testing the Communication

Now, let's test the communication between the two services.

1. Start the **Payment Service** on port 4000:

    bash

    ```
    node paymentService.js
    ```

2. Start the **Order Service** on port 3000:

    bash

    ```
    node orderService.js
    ```

3. Send a POST request to the **Order Service** to create an order and process payment:

    bash

    ```
    curl -X POST http://localhost:3000/orders
    -H "Content-Type: application/json" -d
    '{"userId": 1, "amount": 100}'
    ```

    If the payment is successful, you should see:

    json

    ```
    {
    ```

```
    "message": "Order created successfully",
    "paymentStatus": "Success"
}
```

If the payment fails (e.g., by sending an invalid amount), you would get:

json

```
{
  "message": "Payment failed",
  "paymentStatus": "Failed"
}
```

Conclusion

In this chapter, we learned how microservices communicate with each other using **synchronous** and **asynchronous** methods. We focused on building **RESTful APIs** for communication between services and created a real-world example where an **Order Service** interacts with a **Payment Service**. This example highlights the simplicity of using RESTful APIs to connect microservices in a synchronous manner. You can use this foundation to create more complex interactions and build scalable microservices architectures.

CHAPTER 8

USING DATABASES WITH MICROSERVICES

In this chapter, we will discuss how microservices interact with databases, focusing on the two main types of databases used in microservices architecture: **SQL (Relational)** and **NoSQL (Non-Relational)**. We will then cover how to connect Node.js with **MongoDB** (a popular NoSQL database) and **Sequelize ORM** (a library for interacting with SQL databases). Finally, we will walk through a real-world example of managing product data for an e-commerce platform.

Types of Databases for Microservices: SQL vs NoSQL

When selecting a database for your microservices, it's important to choose one that aligns with your service's requirements. Here are the two most commonly used types of databases:

1. **SQL (Relational Databases)**:
    o **Characteristics**: SQL databases store data in tables with rows and columns, using structured query language (SQL) for querying. These databases enforce relationships between tables, and data is usually stored in a structured format.

- o **Examples**: MySQL, PostgreSQL, SQL Server, SQLite.
- o **Use Cases**: SQL databases are ideal for applications that require complex queries, transactions, and referential integrity (e.g., banking systems, inventory systems).
- o **Advantages**:
  - Strong consistency and ACID compliance (Atomicity, Consistency, Isolation, Durability).
  - Well-suited for applications with structured data and complex relationships.
- o **Disadvantages**:
  - Scalability can be a challenge, especially with large datasets.
  - Not ideal for unstructured or semi-structured data.

2. **NoSQL (Non-Relational Databases)**:
   - o **Characteristics**: NoSQL databases are schema-less and allow for flexible, unstructured data storage. They store data in various formats such as key-value pairs, documents, or graphs.
   - o **Examples**: MongoDB, Cassandra, CouchDB, Redis.

o **Use Cases**: NoSQL databases are often used for applications that require horizontal scaling, unstructured or semi-structured data, and high availability (e.g., social media apps, real-time analytics).

o **Advantages**:

- Highly scalable and flexible with large volumes of data.
- Can handle unstructured data and schema-less storage.

o **Disadvantages**:

- Often lacks ACID compliance, so consistency can be sacrificed in favor of scalability (eventual consistency).
- Not ideal for complex queries or relational data.

Connecting Node.js with a MongoDB Database

MongoDB is a widely used NoSQL database that stores data in a flexible, document-oriented format. We can interact with MongoDB in Node.js using the **Mongoose** library, which provides an easy-to-use API for managing database models and operations.

1. Install MongoDB and Mongoose: First, ensure that MongoDB is installed and running on your machine, or you can use a cloud instance (e.g., MongoDB Atlas).

Next, install Mongoose in your Node.js project:

```bash
npm install mongoose
```

2. Connect to MongoDB: Create a new file called db.js to establish a connection with MongoDB:

```javascript
const mongoose = require('mongoose');

mongoose.connect('mongodb://localhost/ecommerce', { useNewUrlParser: true, useUnifiedTopology: true })
  .then(() => console.log('Connected to MongoDB...'))
  .catch(err => console.error('Could not connect to MongoDB...', err));
```

This code connects to a local MongoDB instance and creates a database named ecommerce. The useNewUrlParser and useUnifiedTopology options are required to avoid deprecation warnings.

3. Define a Schema: Create a model for your product data using Mongoose's schema system.

```javascript
const mongoose = require('mongoose');

const productSchema = new mongoose.Schema({
  name: { type: String, required: true },
  description: String,
  price: { type: Number, required: true },
  category: String,
  stockQuantity: { type: Number, default: 0 }
});

const Product = mongoose.model('Product', productSchema);
module.exports = Product;
```

This schema defines a `Product` model with fields such as `name`, `description`, `price`, `category`, and `stockQuantity`. Mongoose will automatically create the corresponding collection (`products`) in MongoDB.

4. Using the Model to Create and Retrieve Data: You can now create and retrieve product data from the database.

- **Create a New Product**:

```javascript
const Product = require('./productModel');
```

89

```
async function createProduct() {
  const newProduct = new Product({
    name: 'Laptop',
    description: 'High-performance laptop',
    price: 1000,
    category: 'Electronics',
    stockQuantity: 50
  });

  await newProduct.save();
  console.log('Product created:', newProduct);
}
```

- **Get All Products**:

javascript

```
async function getAllProducts() {
  const products = await Product.find();
  console.log('All Products:', products);
}
```

Using Sequelize ORM for Relational Databases

Sequelize is a promise-based Node.js ORM (Object Relational Mapping) for SQL databases. It allows you to interact with a relational database (like MySQL or PostgreSQL) using JavaScript objects, abstracting the complexities of raw SQL queries.

1. Install Sequelize and a Database Driver:

```bash
bash

npm install sequelize mysql2
```

Here, we install `sequelize` (the ORM) and `mysql2` (the driver for MySQL). You can use `pg` for PostgreSQL or `sqlite3` for SQLite.

2. Set Up Sequelize: In a file called `db.js`, we can configure Sequelize to connect to the MySQL database:

```javascript
javascript

const { Sequelize } = require('sequelize');

// Connect to MySQL database
const sequelize = new Sequelize('ecommerce',
'username', 'password', {
  host: 'localhost',
  dialect: 'mysql'
});

// Test the connection
async function testConnection() {
  try {
    await sequelize.authenticate();
```

```
    console.log('Connection to MySQL established
successfully.');
  } catch (error) {
    console.error('Unable to connect to MySQL:',
error);
  }
}


testConnection();
```

3. Define a Model: Now, we can define a product model using Sequelize:

```javascript
const { DataTypes } = require('sequelize');
const sequelize = require('./db');

// Define Product model
const Product = sequelize.define('Product', {
  name: {
    type: DataTypes.STRING,
    allowNull: false
  },
  description: {
    type: DataTypes.STRING
  },
  price: {
    type: DataTypes.FLOAT,
    allowNull: false
```

```
  },
  category: {
    type: DataTypes.STRING
  },
  stockQuantity: {
    type: DataTypes.INTEGER,
    defaultValue: 0
  }
});
```

```
module.exports = Product;
```

4. Sync the Model and Use It: Finally, sync the model and use it to create and retrieve data.

```javascript
const Product = require('./productModel');

// Sync database tables
async function syncDatabase() {
  await sequelize.sync();
  console.log('Database synced');
}

// Create a new product
async function createProduct() {
  const product = await Product.create({
    name: 'Phone',
    description: 'Latest model smartphone',
```

93

```
    price: 700,
    category: 'Electronics',
    stockQuantity: 100
  });
  console.log('Product created:', product);
}


// Get all products
async function getAllProducts() {
  const products = await Product.findAll();
  console.log('Products:', products);
}
```

Real-World Example: Managing Product Data for an E-Commerce Platform

Let's now create a simple **Product Service** for an e-commerce platform where products are managed using a database. We'll use **MongoDB** (NoSQL) for our product database in this example, but the steps are very similar if you were using a relational database with Sequelize.

1. **Product Routes**: Define routes to create and get products in the `productRoutes.js` file.

```javascript
const express = require('express');
const Product = require('./productModel'); // Mongoose model for MongoDB
```

```javascript
const router = express.Router();

// POST route to create a new product
router.post('/products', async (req, res) => {
  try {
    const product = new Product(req.body);
    await product.save();
    res.status(201).json({ message: 'Product created successfully', product });
  } catch (err) {
    res.status(400).json({ error: 'Error creating product' });
  }
});

// GET route to fetch all products
router.get('/products', async (req, res) => {
  try {
    const products = await Product.find();
    res.status(200).json(products);
  } catch (err) {
    res.status(500).json({ error: 'Error fetching products' });
  }
});

module.exports = router;
```

2. **Connect Routes to Express Application**: In your main app.js, connect the routes and start the server.

```javascript
const express = require('express');
const mongoose = require('mongoose');
const productRoutes = require('./productRoutes');

const app = express();
app.use(express.json());

// MongoDB connection
mongoose.connect('mongodb://localhost/ecommerce', { useNewUrlParser: true, useUnifiedTopology: true })
  .then(() => console.log('Connected to MongoDB...'))
  .catch(err => console.error('Error connecting to MongoDB:', err));

// Use product routes
app.use('/api', productRoutes);

const port = 3000;
app.listen(port, () => {
  console.log(`Product Service running on http://localhost:${port}`);
```

```
});
```

Conclusion

In this chapter, we covered the essential concepts of databases in microservices. We explored the differences between **SQL and NoSQL databases** and demonstrated how to connect a Node.js application to **MongoDB** (using Mongoose) and a **relational database** (using Sequelize). The real-world example of managing product data for an e-commerce platform showed how to implement database operations like creating and retrieving products in both types of databases. This chapter has provided you with the foundation to choose the right database for your microservices and integrate it into your Node.js applications.

CHAPTER 9

ERROR HANDLING AND LOGGING IN MICROSERVICES

Error handling and logging are critical aspects of any microservices architecture, as they allow you to identify issues quickly, ensure the system remains resilient, and track the behavior of your services over time. In this chapter, we will explore strategies for error handling in Node.js, setting up logging with popular libraries like **Winston** or **Morgan**, and understanding how errors propagate across microservices. We'll also cover a real-world example of implementing centralized error handling in an application.

Strategies for Error Handling in Node.js

Effective error handling is crucial for maintaining the stability and reliability of your microservices. In Node.js, error handling can be done through a combination of synchronous and asynchronous mechanisms.

1. **Synchronous Error Handling**: In a synchronous context, you typically use **try-catch** blocks to catch exceptions and handle errors.

```javascript

try {
  const            result            =
someFunctionThatMayThrowError();
  console.log(result);
} catch (error) {
  console.error('Error occurred:', error);
}
```

However, this only applies to synchronous code. For asynchronous operations, you'll need to use other strategies.

2. **Asynchronous Error Handling**: Node.js's asynchronous operations, like database queries or HTTP requests, can throw errors that need to be handled using **callback functions** or **Promises**.

   o **Callback-based error handling**: In traditional Node.js APIs, errors are often passed to the callback function as the first argument.

   ```javascript

   fs.readFile('file.txt', (err, data)
   => {
     if (err) {
       console.error('File        read
   error:', err);
   ```

```
    return;
  }
  console.log(data);
});
```

o **Promise-based error handling**: Modern Node.js code often uses Promises for better error management and chaining. You can use `.catch()` to handle errors in Promises:

javascript

```
someAsyncFunction()
  .then(result            =>
console.log(result))
  .catch(error            =>
console.error('Error    occurred:',
error));
```

o **Async/Await-based error handling**: For better readability, async/await syntax is often used to handle errors with `try-catch`:

javascript

```
async function fetchData() {
  try {
    const     data    =    await
fetchSomeData();
```

```
    console.log(data);
} catch (error) {
    console.error('Error      fetching
data:', error);
    }
}
```

3. **Global Error Handling**: It is also essential to implement global error handling for unhandled exceptions and promise rejections. This is especially important in a microservices architecture, where unhandled errors can lead to service crashes.

   o **Handling unhandled promise rejections**: Node.js allows you to handle unhandled promise rejections globally using the `process` object:

   `javascript`

   ```javascript
   process.on('unhandledRejection',
   (reason, promise) => {
     console.error('Unhandled Rejection
   at:', promise, 'reason:', reason);
   });
   ```

   o **Handling uncaught exceptions**: Similarly, uncaught exceptions (synchronous errors that aren't caught) can be handled globally as well:

   `javascript`

```
process.on('uncaughtException',
(error) => {
  console.error('Uncaught
exception:', error);
  process.exit(1);    // Exit the
process after logging the error
});
```

Setting Up Logging with Winston or Morgan

Logging is essential for monitoring the health of your microservices and debugging issues in production. Popular logging libraries for Node.js include **Winston** and **Morgan**.

1. **Winston**: Winston is a versatile logging library that allows you to log messages to different transports (console, files, external services) with various log levels (info, error, warn, etc.).

   o **Installation**:

   bash

   ```
   npm install winston
   ```

   o **Setting Up Winston**: Here's a basic setup for logging with Winston:

   javascript

```
const winston = require('winston');

const              logger              =
winston.createLogger({
  level: 'info',  // Set the default
log level
  transports: [
    new winston.transports.Console({
format: winston.format.simple() }),
    new    winston.transports.File({
filename: 'combined.log' })
  ]
});

// Example usage
logger.info('Informational
message');
logger.error('Error occurred');
```

o **Customizing Log Formats**: You can customize
the log format by using the format property in
the transport setup. For example, using
timestamp and json format for logs:

```
javascript
```

```
const              logger              =
winston.createLogger({
  level: 'info',
```

103

```
format: winston.format.combine(
  winston.format.timestamp(),
  winston.format.json()
),
transports: [
  new
winston.transports.Console(),
  new    winston.transports.File({
filename: 'logs/app.log' })
  ]
});
```

2. **Morgan**: Morgan is a simple HTTP request logger middleware for Node.js. It's great for logging incoming HTTP requests.

    o **Installation**:

    bash

    ```
    npm install morgan
    ```

    o **Setting Up Morgan**: To use Morgan in an Express application, add it as middleware to log every incoming HTTP request:

    javascript

    ```
    const express = require('express');
    const morgan = require('morgan');
    ```

```
const app = express();

app.use(morgan('combined'));  // Log
in 'combined' format (default Apache
log format)

app.get('/', (req, res) => {
  res.send('Hello, world!');
});

app.listen(3000, () => {
  console.log('Server is running on
port 3000');
});
```

3. The 'combined' format logs requests in the Apache-style log format, which includes status code, request method, and other useful information for debugging.

Understanding Error Propagation Between Services

In a microservices architecture, services often need to communicate with each other over APIs (e.g., RESTful APIs). When an error occurs in one service, it's important to propagate that error to the calling service so it can be handled properly.

1. **Error Handling in Synchronous Communication**: If a service makes a synchronous HTTP request to another

service, it can handle errors through standard HTTP response codes. For example:

- o **400 Bad Request**: The request to the service was malformed.
- o **500 Internal Server Error**: The service encountered an unexpected issue.

Example:

javascript

```
app.post('/orders', async (req, res) => {
  try {
    const    paymentResponse    =    await
axios.post('http://payment-
service/process', req.body);
    if (paymentResponse.status === 200) {
      res.status(201).send('Order  created
successfully');
    }
  } catch (error) {
    console.error('Payment         Service
Error:', error);
    res.status(500).send('Error processing
payment');
  }
});
```

2. **Error Handling in Asynchronous Communication**: When using asynchronous communication (e.g., message queues or event-driven systems), error handling often involves retrying failed requests or sending error notifications through an event or message queue.

   o For example, if an order service publishes an event to a queue for payment processing, the payment service could send an acknowledgment or error message back, which the order service processes.

Real-World Example: Implementing Centralized Error Handling in an App

A robust error handling strategy often includes **centralized error handling**, which catches and processes errors consistently across your application.

1. **Create an Error Handling Middleware**: In an Express application, you can set up centralized error handling by adding a middleware that catches all unhandled errors.

```javascript
const express = require('express');
const app = express();

// Sample route that throws an error
```

```
app.get('/', (req, res) => {
  throw   new   Error('Something   went
wrong!');
});

// Centralized error handling middleware
app.use((err, req, res, next) => {
  console.error('Unhandled error:', err);
  res.status(500).json({
    message: 'Something went wrong. Please
try again later.'
  });
});

app.listen(3000, () => {
  console.log('Server is running on port
3000');
});
```

In this example, any unhandled errors are passed to the centralized error handler, which logs the error and sends a generic message to the client. This ensures that your services don't leak sensitive error details to the client, improving security.

2. **Using Winston for Centralized Logging**: We can enhance the above error handler to log the error using Winston:

```javascript

const winston = require('winston');

const logger = winston.createLogger({
  level: 'info',
  transports: [
    new winston.transports.Console(),
    new            winston.transports.File({
filename: 'logs/error.log', level: 'error'
})
  ]
});

app.use((err, req, res, next) => {
  logger.error('Error   occurred:',   err);
// Log the error with Winston
  res.status(500).json({
    message: 'Something went wrong. Please
try again later.'
  });
});
```

Now, every error is logged into the error.log file,
ensuring you can track and review all critical failures in
your application.

Conclusion

In this chapter, we covered essential strategies for **error handling** and **logging** in Node.js microservices. We explored various approaches to handling errors in both synchronous and asynchronous communication, and learned how to set up logging with **Winston** and **Morgan**. Finally, we looked at how errors propagate between services and how to implement **centralized error handling** in a microservice architecture. With this knowledge, you can ensure that your microservices are robust, resilient, and easier to maintain.

CHAPTER 10

AUTHENTICATION AND AUTHORIZATION

In this chapter, we will explore the crucial concepts of **authentication** and **authorization** in microservices. These are key to ensuring that only authorized users can access your services and perform specific actions. We will begin with an introduction to **JWT (JSON Web Tokens)**, which is a popular method for handling authentication in modern applications. Then, we will dive into implementing **user authentication** in microservices, managing **roles and permissions** with **OAuth**, and conclude with a real-world example of securing a login service using JWT.

Introduction to JWT (JSON Web Tokens)

JSON Web Tokens (JWT) is an open standard used for securely transmitting information between parties as a JSON object. JWTs are often used for **authentication** and **information exchange**. They allow the server to verify the user's identity and grant access to protected resources without the need for storing session information on the server.

A JWT consists of three parts:

111

1. **Header**: Contains metadata about the token, such as the signing algorithm (e.g., HMAC, RSA).

2. **Payload**: Contains the claims (i.e., the user's data), such as the user ID or roles.

3. **Signature**: Used to verify that the token has not been tampered with. It is created by signing the header and payload with a secret key.

Structure of a JWT:

css

```
header.payload.signature
```

- **Header**: Encodes information about the signing algorithm and token type (JWT).
- **Payload**: Contains claims (e.g., user data, expiration time).
- **Signature**: Ensures the token's authenticity.

JWT Example:

json

```json
{
  "header": {
    "alg": "HS256",
    "typ": "JWT"
  },
```

```
"payload": {
  "sub": "1234567890",
  "name": "John Doe",
  "iat": 1516239022
},
"signature":
"eyJhbGciOiJIUzI1NiIsInR5cCI6IkpXVCJ9.eyJzdWIiO
iIxMjM0NTY3ODkwIiwibmFtZSI6IkpvaG4gRG9lIiwiaWF0
IjoxNTE2MjM5MDIyfQ.SflKxwRJSMeKKF2QT4fwpMeJf36P
Ok6yJV_adQssw5c"
}
```

JWT Use Cases:

- **Authentication**: After a user logs in, a server generates a JWT and sends it to the client. The client stores the token (usually in local storage or cookies) and sends it back with every subsequent request. The server verifies the token to authenticate the user.

- **Authorization**: The server can include claims (such as user roles) in the JWT payload, enabling the client to determine which resources the user can access.

Implementing User Authentication in Microservices

User authentication is the process of verifying that users are who they claim to be. In microservices, authentication often involves **JWT**. Here's how to implement user authentication in Node.js with **JWT**:

1. **Install Dependencies**: You'll need the following npm packages:

   o **jsonwebtoken**: To generate and verify JWT tokens.

   o **bcryptjs**: To hash passwords for secure storage.

   Install them via npm:

   ```bash
   npm install jsonwebtoken bcryptjs
   ```

2. **User Model**: We will assume that the user data is stored in a MongoDB database using **Mongoose**. Let's define a simple user schema that includes the username and password.

   ```javascript
   const mongoose = require('mongoose');

   const userSchema = new mongoose.Schema({
     username: { type: String, required: true,
   unique: true },
     password: { type: String, required: true
   }
   });
   ```

```
const    User   =    mongoose.model('User',
userSchema);
module.exports = User;
```

3. **User Registration**: When a user registers, we hash their password using `bcryptjs` before saving it to the database.

```
javascript
```

```javascript
const bcrypt = require('bcryptjs');
const User = require('./userModel');

async function registerUser(req, res) {
  const { username, password } = req.body;

  const      hashedPassword      =      await
bcrypt.hash(password,   10);   //   Hash   the
password

  const newUser = new User({ username,
password: hashedPassword });
  await newUser.save();

  res.status(201).send('User    registered
successfully');
}
```

4. **User Login**: When a user logs in, we verify the password using bcryptjs, and if it's correct, we generate a JWT for them.

```javascript
const jwt = require('jsonwebtoken');

async function loginUser(req, res) {
  const { username, password } = req.body;
  const user = await User.findOne({ username });

  if (!user) {
    return res.status(400).send('Invalid credentials');
  }

  const isMatch = await bcrypt.compare(password, user.password);
  if (!isMatch) {
    return res.status(400).send('Invalid credentials');
  }

  // Generate JWT
  const token = jwt.sign({ userId: user._id }, 'your-secret-key', { expiresIn: '1h' });
```

```
res.json({ token });
}
```

In this code:

- o **jwt.sign()**: Generates a JWT containing the user's ID (user._id). The token is signed with a secret key and set to expire in 1 hour.
- o The **token** is sent back to the client, which stores it and sends it in future requests for authentication.

5. **Protecting Routes with JWT**: To protect certain routes, we create middleware that verifies the JWT sent by the client.

```javascript
const jwt = require('jsonwebtoken');

function authenticate(req, res, next) {
  const               token               =
req.header('Authorization')?.replace('Bea
rer ', ''); // Extract token from header

  if (!token) {
    return    res.status(401).send('Access
denied. No token provided.');
  }
```

117

```
try {
    const   decoded   =   jwt.verify(token,
'your-secret-key'); // Verify the token
    req.user = decoded; // Attach the
decoded user data to the request
    next();   //   Proceed   to   the   next
middleware/route
  } catch (err) {
    res.status(400).send('Invalid token');
  }
}
```

You can use this middleware to protect routes like this:

```javascript
```

```javascript
app.get('/profile',   authenticate,   (req,
res) => {
    res.send(`Hello ${req.user.userId}`);
});
```

Managing Roles and Permissions with OAuth

OAuth 2.0 is a protocol that allows third-party applications to access user resources without exposing their credentials. It's often used in conjunction with JWT for **authorization** (e.g., defining user roles and permissions).

1. **OAuth Flow**:

o The user is redirected to an authorization server, where they log in and grant permissions.

o The authorization server issues an **access token** that the client can use to access protected resources.

2. **Managing Roles**: When implementing OAuth, roles and permissions are often managed using scopes. For example, an admin may have a broader set of scopes than a regular user.

Example:

o **Admin Scope**: Allows access to all resources.

o **User Scope**: Allows access to only personal data.

3. **Example of Role-Based Authorization**:

```javascript

function authorizeRoles(roles) {
  return (req, res, next) => {
    if (!roles.includes(req.user.role)) {
      return  res.status(403).send('Access
denied');
    }
    next();
  };
}
```

119

```
app.get('/admin',                     authenticate,
authorizeRoles(['admin']), (req, res) => {
  res.send('Welcome, admin!');
});
```

In this example, the `authorizeRoles` middleware checks if the logged-in user has the required role(s) to access the resource.

Real-World Example: Securing a Login Service with JWT

Now, let's tie everything together into a real-world example: a **Login Service** that authenticates users with JWT. The service will:

- Accept user credentials.
- Hash the password and compare it to the stored hash.
- Generate a JWT token upon successful login.
- Protect certain routes with JWT authentication.

1. **Server Setup**:

javascript

```javascript
const express = require('express');
const bcrypt = require('bcryptjs');
const jwt = require('jsonwebtoken');
const User = require('./userModel');
const { authenticate } = require('./middleware');
```

```
const app = express();
app.use(express.json());

app.post('/login', async (req, res) => {
  const { username, password } = req.body;
  const user = await User.findOne({ username });

  if (!user) {
    return          res.status(400).send('Invalid
credentials');
  }

  const isMatch = await bcrypt.compare(password,
user.password);
  if (!isMatch) {
    return          res.status(400).send('Invalid
credentials');
  }

  // Generate JWT
  const token = jwt.sign({ userId: user._id,
role: 'user' }, 'your-secret-key', { expiresIn:
'1h' });

  res.json({ token });
});

app.get('/profile', authenticate, (req, res) =>
{
```

121

```
    res.send(`Welcome, user ${req.user.userId}`);
});

const port = 3000;
app.listen(port, () => {
    console.log(`Login    Service    running    on
http://localhost:${port}`);
});
```

2. **Testing the Login**:

- Send a **POST** request to `/login` with a valid `username`
  and `password` to get the JWT.
- Use the returned token to authenticate and access
  protected routes like `/profile`.

Conclusion

In this chapter, we covered **authentication** and **authorization** in microservices using **JWT** for user authentication and **OAuth** for role-based access management. We implemented user login with JWT, where the server issues a token that the client can use for subsequent requests. We also explored securing routes with JWT authentication and managing roles with OAuth. By following these practices, you can ensure secure access to your microservices, enabling controlled access based on user roles and permissions.

CHAPTER 11

INTRODUCTION TO SERVICE DISCOVERY

In a microservices architecture, multiple services work together to form a complete application. One of the key challenges in such an architecture is ensuring that each service can find and communicate with the others efficiently. This is where **service discovery** comes into play. In this chapter, we will introduce the concept of service discovery, explore tools like **Consul** and **Eureka** for service discovery, set up a simple service registry with **Node.js**, and walk through a real-world example of dynamically locating microservices in your app.

What is Service Discovery in Microservices?

Service discovery is the process by which microservices automatically detect and locate each other in a dynamic environment. In a traditional monolithic application, communication between components is straightforward, as everything is running within a single application. However, in a microservices architecture, services are often distributed across different servers, containers, or cloud instances. Service discovery ensures that each microservice can dynamically locate the others, enabling smooth communication between them.

124

There are two types of service discovery:

1. **Client-Side Discovery**: In this approach, the client (or consumer of the service) is responsible for locating the appropriate service instance. The client uses a service registry to find the location of services.

2. **Server-Side Discovery**: Here, the client makes requests to a load balancer or API gateway, which queries the service registry to locate the appropriate service instance. The load balancer then forwards the request to the chosen service.

Why is Service Discovery Important?

- **Dynamic Environments**: Microservices often run in dynamic environments where instances can be added or removed, such as in containerized environments (e.g., Docker) or cloud platforms (e.g., AWS, Kubernetes). Service discovery helps manage these changes automatically.

- **Fault Tolerance**: Service discovery enables microservices to be resilient. If one instance of a service fails, the service discovery mechanism can redirect traffic to other healthy instances.

- **Scalability**: As the number of services and instances grows, service discovery ensures that communication between services remains efficient without requiring manual intervention.

Using Tools Like Consul or Eureka for Service Discovery

There are several tools available to implement service discovery in microservices, with **Consul** and **Eureka** being among the most popular:

1. **Consul** (by HashiCorp):
   - **Overview**: Consul is a widely used service discovery and configuration tool. It provides features like health checks, key-value stores, and multi-datacenter support.
   - **How It Works**: Services register themselves with Consul by sending their information (e.g., IP address, port) to the Consul server. Services that want to consume other services query Consul to discover the location of the desired service.
   - **Features**:
     - Service registration and deregistration.
     - Health checks to monitor service availability.
     - Key-value storage for configurations.
2. **Eureka** (by Netflix):
   - **Overview**: Eureka is a service registry that provides service discovery capabilities for the

Spring Cloud ecosystem. It is primarily used in Java-based microservices but can be used with any programming language.

o **How It Works**: Similar to Consul, services register with the Eureka server and periodically send heartbeats to maintain their registration. Clients can query the Eureka server to locate available service instances.

Choosing Between Consul and Eureka:

- **Consul** is more versatile and language-agnostic, supporting many types of services and use cases.
- **Eureka** is more tightly integrated with Spring-based applications, making it ideal for Java-based microservices.

Setting Up a Simple Service Registry with Node.js

Now that we've introduced service discovery tools, let's set up a basic **service registry** using Node.js. We'll implement a simple service registry system where microservices can register themselves, and others can query the registry to discover available services.

1. Install Dependencies: We'll need to install **express** for creating the service registry API and **node-fetch** to simulate service discovery.

127

bash

```
npm install express node-fetch
```

2. Create the Service Registry: Create a file called serviceRegistry.js. This will act as the registry server, where microservices can register and discover each other.

javascript

```javascript
const express = require('express');
const app = express();
const PORT = 3000;


let services = [];  // Store registered services


// Middleware to parse JSON bodies
app.use(express.json());


// Route to register a service
app.post('/register', (req, res) => {
  const { name, url } = req.body;
  if (!name || !url) {
    return  res.status(400).send('Service  name
and URL are required');
  }


  // Add service to the registry
  services.push({ name, url });
```

```
  console.log(`Service  registered:  ${name}  at
${url}`);
  res.status(201).send('Service        registered
successfully');
});

// Route to get all registered services
app.get('/services', (req, res) => {
  res.status(200).json(services);
});

// Route to get a specific service by name
app.get('/services/:name', (req, res) => {
  const service = services.find(s => s.name ===
req.params.name);
  if (!service) {
    return  res.status(404).send('Service  not
found');
  }
  res.status(200).json(service);
});

app.listen(PORT, () => {
  console.log(`Service  Registry  running  on
http://localhost:${PORT}`);
});
```

This serviceRegistry.js file implements:

- **Service registration** via `POST` `/register`, where services can send their `name` and `URL` to be registered.
- **Service discovery** via `GET` `/services` to list all registered services, and `GET` `/services/:name` to get the URL of a specific service.

3. Register and Discover Services:

- To register a service, send a `POST` request with the service name and URL:

bash

```
curl              -X              POST
http://localhost:3000/register        -H
"Content-Type:    application/json"    -d
'{"name":    "payment-service",    "url":
"http://localhost:4000"}'
```

- To discover all registered services, send a `GET` request:

bash

```
curl http://localhost:3000/services
```

This service registry allows microservices to dynamically register themselves and later discover each other by querying the registry.

Real-World Example: Dynamically Locating Microservices in Your App

In a production environment, services often need to find and communicate with each other. In this real-world example, we'll demonstrate how to dynamically discover the **Payment Service** and communicate with it from the **Order Service**.

1. **Order Service**: The **Order Service** will query the service registry to locate the **Payment Service** and send payment requests.

   ```javascript
   const fetch = require('node-fetch');
   const express = require('express');
   const app = express();
   const PORT = 3001;

   app.use(express.json());

   // Function to get the Payment Service URL
   from the Service Registry
   async function getPaymentService() {
     const         response       =         await
   fetch('http://localhost:3000/services/pay
   ment-service');
     const data = await response.json();
     return data.url;
   ```

131

```
}

// Route to create an order and make
payment
app.post('/orders', async (req, res) => {
  const { userId, amount } = req.body;

  try {
    // Dynamically find Payment Service
    const paymentServiceUrl = await
getPaymentService();

    // Make payment request to Payment
Service
    const paymentResponse = await
fetch(`${paymentServiceUrl}/process`, {
      method: 'POST',
      headers: { 'Content-Type':
'application/json' },
      body: JSON.stringify({ userId,
amount })
    });

    if (paymentResponse.status === 200) {
      res.status(201).send('Order created
and payment successful');
    } else {
      res.status(400).send('Payment
failed');
```

```
    }
  } catch (error) {
    res.status(500).send('Error connecting
to Payment Service');
  }
});

app.listen(PORT, () => {
  console.log(`Order  Service  running  on
http://localhost:${PORT}`);
});
```

2. **Payment Service**: The **Payment Service** will have a simple endpoint to simulate processing payments.

```javascript
const express = require('express');
const app = express();
const PORT = 4000;

app.use(express.json());

app.post('/process', (req, res) => {
  const { userId, amount } = req.body;
  // Simulate payment processing
  if (amount > 0) {
    res.status(200).send('Payment
processed successfully');
  } else {
```

```
      res.status(400).send('Invalid  payment
amount');
  }
});
```

```
app.listen(PORT, () => {
  console.log(`Payment Service running on
http://localhost:${PORT}`);
});
```

3. **Testing the Communication**:

    o   Start the **Service Registry** on port 3000.

    o   Register the **Payment Service** in the registry:

    bash

    ```
    curl            -X            POST
    http://localhost:3000/register   -H
    "Content-Type: application/json" -d
    '{"name": "payment-service", "url":
    "http://localhost:4000"}'
    ```

    o   Start the **Order Service** on port 3001.

    o   Create an order by sending a POST request to the
        Order Service:

    bash

```
curl              -X             POST
http://localhost:3001/orders      -H
"Content-Type: application/json" -d
'{"userId": 1, "amount": 100}'
```

The **Order Service** will dynamically locate the **Payment Service** using the service registry and proceed with the payment.

Conclusion

In this chapter, we introduced the concept of **service discovery** in microservices and demonstrated how to use tools like **Consul** or **Eureka** for service registration and discovery. We also created a simple service registry using **Node.js** and implemented a real-world example where one microservice dynamically discovers and interacts with another. Service discovery is essential for managing microservices in dynamic environments, enabling seamless communication and efficient scaling. With this foundation, you can now build more complex, dynamic, and scalable microservices architectures.

CHAPTER 12

INTER-SERVICE COMMUNICATION WITH MESSAGE BROKERS

In a microservices architecture, services often need to communicate with each other to complete complex workflows. While RESTful APIs (synchronous communication) are often used, **asynchronous communication** can be more effective in certain scenarios. One of the key tools for asynchronous communication between microservices is the **message broker**. In this chapter, we will explore message queues, specifically **RabbitMQ** and **Kafka**, and how to use them for inter-service communication. We will then set up a message broker with **Node.js** and walk through a real-world example of implementing an event-driven architecture with **Kafka**.

Understanding Message Queues: RabbitMQ vs Kafka

Message brokers like **RabbitMQ** and **Kafka** are used to handle asynchronous communication between services by sending messages (events or data) to queues. These systems help decouple services, allowing them to communicate without waiting for an immediate response, which increases the resilience and scalability of the system.

1. **RabbitMQ**:
   o **Overview**: RabbitMQ is a message broker that uses a traditional message queue model based on the Advanced Message Queuing Protocol (AMQP). It allows for message delivery guarantees such as message persistence, acknowledgments, and retries.

   o **Use Cases**: RabbitMQ is ideal for scenarios that require guaranteed message delivery and where the messages are processed in a sequential or prioritized manner.

   o **Features**:
   - **Queues**: Messages are stored in queues until they are consumed by services.
   - **Exchanges**: Routes messages to queues based on routing rules.
   - **Reliable Delivery**: Ensures messages are not lost even if a consumer is down.
   - **Message Acknowledgments**: Ensures messages are acknowledged by consumers.

   o **When to Use**:
   - Workflows where services need to process messages in a guaranteed order.

- Reliable communication where message delivery is crucial.

2. **Kafka**:

   o **Overview**: Kafka is a distributed event streaming platform that can be used as a message broker. Unlike RabbitMQ, Kafka is built around a **publish-subscribe** model where services produce (publish) events and other services consume them.

   o **Use Cases**: Kafka is well-suited for high-throughput, real-time event streaming and large-scale data processing. It's commonly used in scenarios like event sourcing, logging, or monitoring.

   o **Features**:

     - **Topics**: Kafka organizes messages into topics (logical message categories).

     - **Consumers and Producers**: Producers send messages to topics, and consumers read messages from topics.

     - **High Throughput**: Kafka can handle very high volumes of messages with low latency.

     - **Durability**: Kafka stores messages in logs, ensuring messages are durable and can be replayed.

o **When to Use**:

- Real-time data streaming or event-driven architectures.
- Systems that need to process large volumes of events with high throughput.

RabbitMQ vs Kafka:

- **RabbitMQ** is more suited for traditional message queuing scenarios with guaranteed delivery and message acknowledgments.
- **Kafka** is more scalable and better for high-throughput, event-driven systems with real-time stream processing.

Setting Up a Message Broker with Node.js

In this section, we will demonstrate how to set up both **RabbitMQ** and **Kafka** for inter-service communication in a Node.js application.

1. Setting Up RabbitMQ with Node.js

1. **Install RabbitMQ**: To install RabbitMQ, follow the installation instructions for your platform on the official website.
2. **Install Required Libraries**: We will use the **amqplib** library to interact with RabbitMQ in Node.js.

```bash
bash

npm install amqplib
```

3. **Producer (Sending Messages)**: Create a `producer.js` file to send messages to RabbitMQ.

```javascript
javascript

const amqp = require('amqplib');

async function sendMessage() {
  const connection = await
amqp.connect('amqp://localhost');
  const channel = await
connection.createChannel();

  const queue = 'task_queue';
  const msg = 'Hello, RabbitMQ!';

  await channel.assertQueue(queue, {
durable: true });
  channel.sendToQueue(queue,
Buffer.from(msg), { persistent: true });

  console.log('Message sent:', msg);
  await channel.close();
  await connection.close();
}
```

```
sendMessage().catch(console.error);
```

4. **Consumer (Receiving Messages)**: Create a consumer.js file to consume messages from RabbitMQ.

```javascript
const amqp = require('amqplib');

async function receiveMessage() {
  const connection = await amqp.connect('amqp://localhost');
  const channel = await connection.createChannel();

  const queue = 'task_queue';

  await channel.assertQueue(queue, { durable: true });
  console.log('Waiting for messages in %s. To exit press CTRL+C', queue);

  channel.consume(queue, (msg) => {
    if (msg !== null) {
      console.log('Received:', msg.content.toString());
      channel.ack(msg);
    }
```

```
});
}
```

```
receiveMessage().catch(console.error);
```

5. **Testing RabbitMQ**:
   - o Run `consumer.js` to listen for messages.
   - o Run `producer.js` to send a message. The consumer will log the received message.

2. Setting Up Kafka with Node.js

1. **Install Kafka**: Kafka requires a running Kafka instance. Follow the instructions on the <u>official Kafka website</u> to install and set up Kafka.

2. **Install Required Libraries**: We'll use the **kafkajs** library to interact with Kafka.

```bash
bash
```

```
npm install kafkajs
```

3. **Producer (Sending Events)**: Create a `kafkaProducer.js` file to send messages to Kafka.

```javascript
javascript
```

```
const { Kafka } = require('kafkajs');
```

142

```
const kafka = new Kafka({
  clientId: 'my-app',
  brokers: ['localhost:9092'],
});

const producer = kafka.producer();

async function sendEvent() {
  await producer.connect();
  await producer.send({
    topic: 'order-events',
    messages: [
      { value: 'Order created with ID 123'
},
    ],
  });
  console.log('Message sent to Kafka');
  await producer.disconnect();
}

sendEvent().catch(console.error);
```

4. **Consumer (Receiving Events)**: Create a kafkaConsumer.js file to consume messages from Kafka.

javascript

```
const { Kafka } = require('kafkajs');
```

143

```
const kafka = new Kafka({
  clientId: 'my-app',
  brokers: ['localhost:9092'],
});

const consumer = kafka.consumer({ groupId:
'order-group' });

async function receiveEvent() {
  await consumer.connect();
  await    consumer.subscribe({    topic:
'order-events', fromBeginning: true });

  await consumer.run({
    eachMessage:    async    ({    topic,
partition, message }) => {
      console.log(`Received        message:
${message.value.toString()}`);
    },
  });
}

receiveEvent().catch(console.error);
```

5. **Testing Kafka**:

   o   Start Kafka by running the Kafka server and
       ensuring ZooKeeper is running.

   o   Run `kafkaConsumer.js` to listen for events.

144

o   **Run** `kafkaProducer.js` to send an event to Kafka. The consumer will log the received message.

Real-World Example: Implementing an Event-Driven Architecture with Kafka

Let's implement a real-world example where we use Kafka for inter-service communication in an event-driven architecture. In this example, when an **Order Service** creates a new order, it will send an event to a **Payment Service** via Kafka. The Payment Service will then process the payment based on the received event.

1. **Order Service (Producer)**: The **Order Service** will publish an event to Kafka whenever a new order is created.

   javascript

```javascript
const { Kafka } = require('kafkajs');

const kafka = new Kafka({
  clientId: 'order-service',
  brokers: ['localhost:9092'],
});

const producer = kafka.producer();
```

```
async       function       createOrder(orderId,
amount) {
  await producer.connect();
  await producer.send({
    topic: 'order-events',
    messages: [
      { value: JSON.stringify({ orderId,
amount }) },
    ],
  });
  console.log(`Order  created:  ${orderId},
amount: ${amount}`);
  await producer.disconnect();
}

createOrder(123,
1000).catch(console.error);
```

2. **Payment Service (Consumer)**: The **Payment Service** will consume the order-events topic to process payments.

```javascript
const { Kafka } = require('kafkajs');

const kafka = new Kafka({
  clientId: 'payment-service',
  brokers: ['localhost:9092'],
```

```
});

const consumer = kafka.consumer({ groupId:
'payment-group' });

async function processPayment() {
  await consumer.connect();
  await     consumer.subscribe({     topic:
'order-events', fromBeginning: true });

  await consumer.run({
    eachMessage:     async     ({     topic,
partition, message }) => {
      const           order          =
JSON.parse(message.value.toString());
      console.log(`Processing payment for
Order    ID:    ${order.orderId},    Amount:
${order.amount}`);
      // Simulate payment processing logic
here
    },
  });
}

processPayment().catch(console.error);
```

3. **Testing Event-Driven Architecture**:
   o Start the **Kafka broker** and make sure ZooKeeper is running.

- o Start the **Payment Service** to listen for events.
- o Run the **Order Service** to create an order. The Payment Service will process the payment after receiving the event.

Conclusion

In this chapter, we introduced **message brokers** as a powerful tool for asynchronous communication in microservices. We explored two popular message brokers—**RabbitMQ** and **Kafka**—and demonstrated how to set up and use them in Node.js for inter-service communication. We then implemented a **real-world event-driven architecture** using Kafka, where services communicate by publishing and consuming events. This approach decouples services, increases resilience, and improves scalability in microservices-based applications. With Kafka or RabbitMQ, you can efficiently implement event-driven patterns in your microservices architecture.

CHAPTER 13

IMPLEMENTING CACHING IN MICROSERVICES

In microservices architectures, performance and scalability are key concerns. One effective way to improve the efficiency of your services and reduce latency is by implementing **caching**. Caching can help minimize the number of expensive operations (such as database queries or API calls) by storing frequently accessed data in memory. In this chapter, we will explore why caching is essential in microservices, introduce **Redis** as a caching solution, discuss different caching strategies, and provide a real-world example of caching product data to improve response times.

Why Use Caching in Microservices?

Caching plays a critical role in enhancing the performance of microservices by reducing response times and improving resource utilization. Below are the main reasons why caching is beneficial in a microservices architecture:

1. **Reduced Latency**: Caching allows frequently accessed data to be retrieved quickly from memory instead of querying a database or making an external API call. This reduces latency, leading to faster response times for users.

2. **Reduced Load on Backend Systems**: By caching data, you can reduce the number of expensive operations that need to be performed on backend systems (like databases, external services, or APIs). This helps reduce load on these systems, improving their overall performance and scalability.

3. **Improved Scalability**: Caching can help your microservices scale more efficiently by reducing the pressure on backend systems, allowing them to handle more requests simultaneously.

4. **Cost Savings**: By reducing the number of calls to databases or other resources, caching can help save on computational costs. For cloud-based services, minimizing the need for expensive database queries or API calls can result in significant cost savings.

5. **Enhanced Fault Tolerance**: Caching also improves the availability and fault tolerance of your services. If the backend system goes down, the cache can serve the data, allowing your service to continue operating without interruption.

Introduction to Redis for Caching

Redis is an open-source, in-memory data structure store that is widely used for caching in microservices. Redis supports various data types, such as strings, hashes, lists, sets, and sorted sets, which makes it highly versatile for different use cases.

Why Redis?

- **In-Memory Storage**: Redis stores data in memory, making it extremely fast compared to traditional disk-based databases.
- **Simple API**: Redis has a simple and efficient API for interacting with data, making it easy to integrate into applications.
- **Persistence**: Although Redis is an in-memory store, it can persist data to disk (optional) for durability.
- **Scalability**: Redis supports clustering, allowing it to scale horizontally across multiple machines.
- **Pub/Sub**: Redis supports publish/subscribe messaging, which is useful in event-driven architectures.

Basic Redis Operations:

- **SET**: Store data in Redis.

  bash

  ```
  SET key value
  ```

- **GET**: Retrieve data from Redis.

  bash

  ```
  GET key
  ```

- **DEL**: Delete a key-value pair from Redis.

bash

```
DEL key
```

Caching Strategies: Cache-aside vs Write-through

There are two common caching strategies used in microservices: **Cache-aside** and **Write-through**. Each strategy has its advantages depending on the use case.

1. **Cache-aside (Lazy-Loading)**:
   o **How It Works**: In this strategy, the application is responsible for loading data into the cache. When data is requested, the application first checks the cache. If the data is not in the cache (a cache miss), it retrieves the data from the backend (e.g., database or external API), stores it in the cache, and returns it to the client.
   o **When to Use**: Cache-aside is ideal when data is read frequently but does not change often. It's a good fit for applications where the cost of data retrieval is high, and it's okay to load data lazily on demand.
   o **Example**: Caching product data in an e-commerce application. When the product data is

requested, it's fetched from the cache if available, or from the database if not.

Advantages:

o   Reduces database load by caching data on demand.

o   Flexible cache eviction policies.

Disadvantages:

o   Cache misses require a database or external API call, which may lead to higher latency.

2. **Write-through (Eager-Loading)**:

o   **How It Works**: In a write-through strategy, data is written to the cache at the same time it is written to the backend. This ensures that the cache is always up-to-date with the latest data.

o   **When to Use**: Write-through is useful when you want to keep the cache in sync with the database and ensure that any changes to the data are immediately reflected in the cache.

o   **Example**: Caching user preferences or session data. Whenever a user updates their preferences, the changes are immediately written to both the database and the cache.

Advantages:

- o Ensures the cache is always in sync with the database.
- o Prevents cache misses for frequently updated data.

Disadvantages:

- o Writing data to both the cache and database can add overhead.
- o Can result in stale data if updates are not properly managed.

Real-World Example: Caching Product Data for Faster Response Times

Let's implement a simple example of caching product data for an e-commerce application using **Redis** and the **Cache-aside** strategy. This will help us reduce the response time for product lookups by caching the product data in memory.

1. Install Redis: If you haven't already, install Redis by following the official installation guide. You can also use managed Redis services like **Redis Labs** or **Amazon ElastiCache**.

2. Install Redis Client for Node.js: Install the **ioredis** library to interact with Redis in Node.js:

bash

```
npm install ioredis
```

3. Set Up Product Service with Caching: Let's create a `productService.js` file that will check the Redis cache for product data before querying the database.

```javascript
const Redis = require('ioredis');
const redis = new Redis();   // Connect to Redis
const express = require('express');
const app = express();
const PORT = 3000;

// Simulated database for products
const productDatabase = {
    1: { id: 1, name: 'Laptop', price: 1000 },
    2: { id: 2, name: 'Phone', price: 500 },
    3: { id: 3, name: 'Headphones', price: 150 },
};

// Function to get product from cache or database
async function getProduct(productId) {
    const         cachedProduct        =         await
redis.get(`product:${productId}`);
    if (cachedProduct) {
        console.log('Cache hit');
```

```
      return JSON.parse(cachedProduct);   // Return
the product from cache
  } else {
    console.log('Cache miss');
    // Simulate a database call
    const product = productDatabase[productId];
    if (product) {
      await    redis.set(`product:${productId}`,
JSON.stringify(product), 'EX', 60);  // Cache for
60 seconds
      return product;
    }
    return null;
  }
}


// Route to fetch product by ID
app.get('/product/:id', async (req, res) => {
  const productId = req.params.id;
  const product = await getProduct(productId);

  if (product) {
    res.status(200).json(product);
  } else {
    res.status(404).send('Product not found');
  }
});


app.listen(PORT, () => {
```

```
console.log(`Product    Service    running    on
http://localhost:${PORT}`);
});
```

Explanation:

- **Redis Cache Check**: When a product is requested, we first check if the product exists in Redis. If found (cache hit), we return the cached data.
- **Database Lookup**: If the product is not found in the cache (cache miss), we simulate a database lookup and then cache the result in Redis for future requests.
- **Cache Expiration**: We set the cache to expire in 60 seconds, meaning after 60 seconds, Redis will automatically remove the cached product data.

4. Testing the Caching:

- Run the application:

```bash
node productService.js
```

- Send a GET request to retrieve a product:

```bash
curl http://localhost:3000/product/1
```

On the first request, the product data will be fetched from the "database" and cached in Redis. Subsequent requests will retrieve the data from Redis, resulting in a faster response time.

Conclusion

In this chapter, we explored the importance of **caching** in microservices to improve performance, reduce latency, and increase scalability. We introduced **Redis** as a popular caching solution and discussed two common caching strategies: **Cache-aside** and **Write-through**. We then demonstrated how to implement caching in a product service using the **Cache-aside** strategy, ensuring faster response times for product lookups. By utilizing Redis and caching strategies, you can significantly enhance the performance of your microservices and optimize system resources.

CHAPTER 14

BUILDING SCALABLE MICROSERVICES WITH LOAD BALANCING

In a microservices architecture, scalability and availability are crucial to handling increased load and ensuring that the system can grow efficiently. One of the key techniques for improving scalability and availability is **load balancing**. In this chapter, we will explore the concept of load balancing, how to set it up using **Nginx** for Node.js applications, and how to implement **horizontal scaling** for microservices. We will also walk through a real-world example of deploying scalable services in the cloud.

What is Load Balancing?

Load balancing is the process of distributing incoming network traffic across multiple servers or instances of an application to ensure that no single server becomes overwhelmed. It helps achieve:

- **Improved availability**: By distributing requests across multiple instances, the system can tolerate the failure of one or more servers without affecting the availability of the service.

- **Better resource utilization**: Load balancing ensures that each server instance handles an appropriate number of requests, preventing underutilization or overloading of any single instance.
- **Scalability**: As traffic increases, you can add more instances of your service and the load balancer will distribute the traffic evenly, allowing the system to scale horizontally.

There are several types of load balancing strategies:

- **Round-robin**: Distributes requests evenly across all available servers.
- **Least connections**: Sends traffic to the server with the least number of active connections.
- **IP Hashing**: Routes requests based on the client's IP address, ensuring that subsequent requests from the same client are directed to the same server.

In a **microservices architecture**, load balancing is critical because multiple instances of a service may be running to handle incoming requests, and the load balancer ensures that these requests are distributed efficiently.

Using Nginx for Load Balancing in Node.js Applications

Nginx is a widely used web server and reverse proxy that can also act as a load balancer. It is highly efficient and can distribute traffic to multiple backend servers running Node.js applications.

1. Installing Nginx: To use Nginx for load balancing, you first need to install Nginx on a server. Follow the instructions for your platform from the official Nginx website.

2. Configuring Nginx as a Load Balancer: Once Nginx is installed, you can configure it to balance the load across multiple Node.js application instances.

Here's how to set up **Nginx** for load balancing:

1. **Edit the Nginx Configuration**: Open the Nginx configuration file (usually found at `/etc/nginx/nginx.conf`) and modify it to include a load balancing setup.

   Example configuration for load balancing:

   ```nginx
   http {
       upstream node_app {
           server 127.0.0.1:3001;  # Instance
   1 of your Node.js app
   ```

```
        server 127.0.0.1:3002;  # Instance
2 of your Node.js app
        server 127.0.0.1:3003;  # Instance
3 of your Node.js app
    }


    server {
        listen 80;  # Listen on port 80 for
incoming requests

        location / {
            proxy_pass http://node_app;  #
Forward requests to Node.js app
            proxy_http_version 1.1;
            proxy_set_header       Upgrade
$http_upgrade;
            proxy_set_header       Connection
'upgrade';
            proxy_set_header Host $host;
            proxy_cache_bypass
$http_upgrade;
        }
    }
}
```

In this configuration:

o **upstream node_app**: Defines the backend services (your Node.js application instances) that Nginx will distribute traffic to.

o **server**: Each `server` directive defines an instance of your Node.js application running on different ports (3001, 3002, 3003 in this case).

o **proxy_pass http://node_app**: The incoming traffic on port 80 is forwarded to the `node_app` upstream group.

2. **Start Nginx**: Once you've updated the configuration file, restart Nginx to apply the changes:

```bash

sudo systemctl restart nginx
```

3. **Testing Load Balancing**:

o Start your Node.js application on different ports (3001, 3002, 3003).

o Send HTTP requests to `http://localhost` and Nginx will distribute them across your Node.js instances.

Setting Up Horizontal Scaling for Node.js Microservices

Horizontal scaling, also known as **scaling out**, involves adding more instances of your services to handle increased traffic. Unlike vertical scaling (increasing the resources of a single instance), horizontal scaling distributes the load across multiple machines or containers.

In this section, we will demonstrate how to horizontally scale your Node.js microservices and use Nginx as a load balancer to distribute requests.

1. Start Multiple Instances of the Node.js Application: To horizontally scale a Node.js application, you can run multiple instances of the same service. In production, this can be achieved using **Docker containers** or **Node.js clustering**.

- **Using Node.js Cluster**: Node.js has a built-in **cluster** module that allows you to take advantage of multi-core systems by creating multiple worker processes. Here's an example of using the cluster module:

javascript

```
const cluster = require('cluster');
const http = require('http');
const os = require('os');
const numCPUs = os.cpus().length;

if (cluster.isMaster) {
  // Fork workers for each CPU core
  for (let i = 0; i < numCPUs; i++) {
    cluster.fork();
  }
```

164

```
cluster.on('exit',      (worker,     code,
signal) => {
   console.log(`Worker
${worker.process.pid} died`);
  });
} else {
  // Worker processes running Node.js app
  http.createServer((req, res) => {
    res.writeHead(200,  {  'Content-Type':
'text/plain' });
    res.end('Hello World');
  }).listen(8000);
}
```

In this example, the **master** process spawns worker processes based on the number of available CPU cores.

- **Using Docker**: You can also scale your services by running multiple instances of your Node.js application in Docker containers. For instance, you could use **Docker Compose** to define and manage multi-container setups.

Example docker-compose.yml:

```yaml
yaml
```

```
version: '3'
services:
```

```
node_app:
    image: node-app
    ports:
        - "3001:3001"
        - "3002:3002"
        - "3003:3003"
```

2. Scale Application in the Cloud: For cloud deployments, horizontal scaling is often managed using cloud services such as **Amazon ECS, Google Kubernetes Engine (GKE)**, or **Azure Kubernetes Service (AKS)**. These platforms allow you to automatically scale the number of instances of your application based on traffic demand.

3. Scaling with Load Balancing: Once you have multiple instances running, **Nginx** (or another load balancer like HAProxy) can distribute traffic across these instances. This setup ensures that the system remains available and responsive as the load increases.

Real-World Example: Deploying Scalable Services in the Cloud

Let's implement a real-world example where we deploy scalable **Node.js microservices** using **AWS Elastic Beanstalk** (or any similar cloud platform) with **Nginx** as the load balancer.

1. **Deploy Node.js Application to AWS Elastic Beanstalk**:
    o   AWS Elastic Beanstalk simplifies the deployment and management of applications.

166

You can deploy Node.js applications by creating an Elastic Beanstalk environment, which automatically provisions the required infrastructure and load balancing.

o   Follow the AWS Elastic Beanstalk Node.js guide to deploy your application.

2. **Configure Auto-Scaling**:

o   AWS Elastic Beanstalk supports auto-scaling, which automatically adjusts the number of instances based on traffic.

o   You can configure auto-scaling by adjusting the environment settings in the AWS Management Console, allowing the number of application instances to grow or shrink based on traffic load.

3. **Set Up Nginx for Load Balancing**:

o   AWS Elastic Load Balancer (ELB) automatically distributes traffic across the deployed instances. However, if you're managing Nginx manually, you can configure it as we described earlier to handle load balancing between instances.

o   You can also configure Nginx to handle SSL termination for secure HTTPS traffic.

4. **Test Scalability**:

o   After deploying and configuring your application, you can test horizontal scaling by simulating increased traffic using tools like

Apache JMeter or **Artillery**. Monitor the performance and ensure that the load is evenly distributed across your instances.

Conclusion

In this chapter, we discussed the importance of **load balancing** and **horizontal scaling** in microservices architectures. We explored how **Nginx** can be used as a load balancer for Node.js applications to distribute traffic across multiple service instances. We also demonstrated how to horizontally scale your microservices by running multiple instances of your Node.js application, either using **Node.js clustering** or **Docker** containers. Finally, we provided a real-world example of deploying scalable services in the cloud using **AWS Elastic Beanstalk**. By implementing these practices, you can build microservices that scale efficiently and handle high traffic loads without compromising performance or availability.

CHAPTER 15

MANAGING MICROSERVICES WITH DOCKER

In a microservices architecture, managing services across different environments can be challenging. One of the most effective solutions is using **containers**, which provide a lightweight and portable way to package applications and their dependencies. In this chapter, we will introduce **Docker** and explain how to use it to containerize **Node.js microservices**. We'll also explore **Docker Compose** for managing multi-container applications. Finally, we will provide a real-world example of **containerizing a Node.js-based user service**.

Introduction to Containers and Docker

A **container** is a lightweight, standalone, executable package that includes everything needed to run a piece of software: the code, runtime, libraries, and dependencies. Containers isolate applications from the underlying host system, making it easier to deploy and run them in different environments (development, testing, production) without compatibility issues.

Docker is an open-source platform used to create, deploy, and run containers. Docker simplifies the process of packaging and

169

distributing applications, ensuring that they work consistently across different environments.

- **Benefits of Containers**:
  - o **Portability**: Containers can run anywhere—on local machines, cloud platforms, or virtual machines—without modification.
  - o **Isolation**: Containers provide process and resource isolation, meaning one service in a container does not interfere with others.
  - o **Efficiency**: Containers share the host system's kernel, making them more efficient in terms of system resources compared to virtual machines.
  - o **Consistency**: Docker ensures that the application runs the same way, regardless of where it is deployed.

Docker provides tools to create and manage containers. Some key Docker components include:

- **Docker Engine**: The core component that runs containers.
- **Docker Images**: A lightweight, standalone, and executable package that includes everything needed to run an application.
- **Docker Containers**: An instance of a Docker image that is running.

Creating Docker Containers for Node.js Microservices

To get started with Docker and containerize a Node.js microservice, we'll follow these basic steps:

1. **Install Docker**:
   o First, ensure Docker is installed on your machine. You can download and install Docker from the official Docker website.
2. **Create a Node.js Application**: Let's start by creating a simple Node.js application to containerize. Here's a basic example of a Node.js app (`app.js`):

```javascript
const express = require('express');
const app = express();
const port = 3000;

app.get('/', (req, res) => {
  res.send('Hello, Docker!');
});

app.listen(port, () => {
  console.log(`App running at http://localhost:${port}`);
});
```

3. **Create a Dockerfile**: A **Dockerfile** is a script that defines how to build a Docker image for your application. It contains instructions to set up the environment, install dependencies, your application files, and start the application.

Here's a simple `Dockerfile` to containerize the Node.js app:

```
Dockerfile

# Use an official Node.js runtime as the
base image
FROM node:14

# Set the working directory inside the
container
WORKDIR /usr/src/app

# package.json and package-lock.json to
the container
 package*.json ./

# Install dependencies
RUN npm install

# the rest of the application files to the
container
  . .
```

172

```
# Expose  port  3000  to  access  the
application
EXPOSE 3000


# Command to run the app
CMD ["node", "app.js"]
```

Explanation:

- o FROM node:14: Uses the official Node.js image as the base image.
- o WORKDIR /usr/src/app: Sets the working directory inside the container.
- o package*.json ./: Copies the package.json and package-lock.json to the container.
- o RUN npm install: Installs the application dependencies inside the container.
- o . .: Copies the rest of the application files to the container.
- o EXPOSE 3000: Exposes port 3000, allowing access to the application running inside the container.
- o CMD ["node", "app.js"]: Defines the command to run the app.

4. **Build the Docker Image**: Once the `Dockerfile` is set up, you can build the Docker image using the following command in the terminal (run it in the same directory as the `Dockerfile`):

bash

```
docker build -t nodejs-app .
```

This command tells Docker to build the image with the tag `nodejs-app` using the current directory (`.`) as the context.

5. **Run the Docker Container**: After the image is built, you can run a container based on the image:

bash

```
docker run -p 3000:3000 nodejs-app
```

This command runs the container and maps port 3000 on the host to port 3000 inside the container, making the application accessible at `http://localhost:3000`.

Docker Compose for Managing Multi-Container Applications

In microservices architectures, multiple services may need to run together, and managing them individually with Docker can become cumbersome. **Docker Compose** is a tool that allows you to define and manage multi-container Docker applications. It simplifies the process of running multiple services together.

1. **Install Docker Compose**: Docker Compose comes with Docker Desktop, but if you're using a different platform, you may need to install it manually. Follow the installation instructions on the Docker Compose documentation.

2. **Create a `docker-compose.yml` File**: Let's set up a simple `docker-compose.yml` file to run multiple services (e.g., a Node.js app and a MongoDB database) in containers.

Here's an example `docker-compose.yml` for running a Node.js app with MongoDB:

```yaml
version: '3'
services:
  app:
    build: .
    ports:
      - "3000:3000"
    depends_on:
      - mongo
  mongo:
    image: mongo
```

```
    volumes:
      - mongo-data:/data/db
    ports:
      - "27017:27017"

volumes:
  mongo-data:
```

Explanation:

- o **services**: Defines the different services in the application.
    - ▪ **app**: The Node.js application, built from the Dockerfile in the current directory (`build: .`).
    - ▪ **mongo**: The MongoDB service, using the official MongoDB image. It stores its data in a named volume (`mongo-data`).
- o **depends_on**: Ensures that the app service starts after the `mongo` service.
- o **volumes**: Defines a named volume to persist MongoDB data.

3. **Start the Services with Docker Compose**: To start the services, simply run the following command:

```bash
docker-compose up
```

Docker Compose will build and start both the `app` and `mongo` services. The Node.js app will be accessible on port 3000, and MongoDB will be running on port 27017.

4. **Scaling Services with Docker Compose**: You can scale services in Docker Compose by increasing the number of containers for a specific service. For example, to scale the `app` service to 3 instances:

```bash
docker-compose up --scale app=3
```

This command starts 3 instances of the Node.js application behind the load balancer.

Real-World Example: Containerizing a Node.js-Based User Service

Let's walk through an example of containerizing a **User Service** that communicates with a database (e.g., MongoDB) in a microservices architecture.

1. **Create the User Service**:
   o Set up a simple Node.js application that provides CRUD operations for user data (this can include user registration, login, etc.).

o For this example, we'll use **MongoDB** for storing user data and the **Mongoose** ORM for interacting with the database.

2. **Dockerize the User Service**:

   o Write a `Dockerfile` to containerize the user service (as shown in the earlier section).

   o Create a `docker-compose.yml` to include both the User Service and MongoDB in containers.

3. **Deploying the Application**:

   o Build and run the services with `docker-compose up`.

   o Access the User Service at `http://localhost:3000` and interact with the user management endpoints.

4. **Scaling the User Service**:

   o If the traffic to the User Service increases, you can scale it horizontally by adding more containers using Docker Compose's `--scale` option. This allows you to handle increased load and ensure high availability.

Conclusion

In this chapter, we explored how to use **Docker** to containerize **Node.js microservices**, which simplifies deployment and management. We also introduced **Docker Compose** for managing multi-container applications and demonstrated how to scale services by running multiple instances. Using **Docker** and **Docker Compose** helps achieve portability, scalability, and consistency, making it easier to deploy and manage microservices. By containerizing services, you can ensure that they run the same way in different environments, from local development to production, and scale them effectively to handle varying levels of traffic.

CHAPTER 16

ORCHESTRATING MICROSERVICES WITH KUBERNETES

As the number of microservices grows, managing and deploying these services efficiently becomes a challenge. **Kubernetes** is the leading container orchestration platform that automates the deployment, scaling, and management of containerized applications. In this chapter, we will explore **Kubernetes**, its role in managing microservices, and how to use it for deploying Node.js applications. We'll also walk through scaling and managing microservices with Kubernetes and provide a real-world example of deploying microservices on **AWS** using Kubernetes.

Introduction to Kubernetes and Its Role in Microservices

Kubernetes (often abbreviated as **K8s**) is an open-source platform for automating the deployment, scaling, and management of containerized applications. It provides a unified system for managing containers, which are often used to deploy microservices in modern application architectures.

Kubernetes is essential for microservices because it offers the following capabilities:

1. **Automated Deployment and Rollouts**:
   o Kubernetes automates the deployment of microservices across clusters of machines. It ensures that your services are deployed consistently and that updates are rolled out without downtime.

2. **Scaling**:
   o Kubernetes allows you to scale your services up or down based on demand. This can be done manually or automatically using metrics like CPU usage or response times.

3. **Self-Healing**:
   o Kubernetes automatically monitors the health of your services and replaces containers that fail or become unresponsive, ensuring high availability.

4. **Service Discovery and Load Balancing**:
   o Kubernetes provides built-in service discovery and load balancing, which ensures that requests are distributed across the available instances of a service.

5. **Resource Management**:
   o Kubernetes efficiently manages resources (like CPU and memory) across your clusters, ensuring

that each service gets the necessary resources without overloading any single node.

6. **Declarative Configuration**:
   o Kubernetes uses configuration files (usually in YAML or JSON format) to declare how applications should be deployed, scaled, and managed. This provides a version-controlled and repeatable way to manage microservices.

Setting Up Kubernetes Clusters for Node.js Applications

To get started with Kubernetes, you'll first need a **Kubernetes cluster** where your Node.js applications can be deployed. A Kubernetes cluster consists of one or more **nodes**, each of which runs containerized applications.

Here's a step-by-step guide to setting up Kubernetes for your Node.js applications:

1. Installing Kubernetes (Minikube for Local Development): For local development, you can use **Minikube**, which provides a local Kubernetes cluster on your machine.

- **Install Minikube**:
  o Follow the installation instructions for Minikube on the official Minikube website.
- **Start a Local Cluster**: Once Minikube is installed, start a Kubernetes cluster by running:

```bash
minikube start
```

- **Verify Kubernetes Installation**: To check the status of your Kubernetes cluster, run:

```bash
kubectl get nodes
```

2. Setting Up Docker and Kubernetes Integration:

- **Docker**: Kubernetes uses Docker (or other container runtimes) to run containers. Make sure Docker is installed on your machine, as Minikube uses it to build and run containers.
- **Kubernetes CLI (kubectl)**: You'll use `kubectl` to interact with your Kubernetes cluster. It's automatically installed with Minikube.

3. Creating a Kubernetes Deployment for Node.js: Kubernetes uses **deployments** to manage the lifecycle of your containers. Here's how you can create a deployment for your Node.js application.

- **Dockerize Your Node.js Application**: If you haven't already, create a Docker image of your Node.js app. For example, here's a simple `Dockerfile` for your Node.js app:

```
Dockerfile

# Use Node.js image as the base
FROM node:14

# Set the working directory inside the
container
WORKDIR /usr/src/app

#  package.json and install dependencies
 package*.json ./
RUN npm install

#  the rest of the application files
 .  .

# Expose the app's port
EXPOSE 3000

# Command to run the app
CMD ["node", "app.js"]
```

- **Build Docker Image**: Build the Docker image for your Node.js application:

```bash
bash
```

```
docker build -t nodejs-app .
```

- **Push Docker Image to a Registry**: You can push the Docker image to Docker Hub or any private container registry:

```
bash
```

```
docker push your-username/nodejs-app
```

4. Creating Kubernetes Configuration Files: Now, create Kubernetes configuration files to define your deployment and service.

- **Deployment YAML**: Create a file called deployment.yaml that defines how your Node.js app will be deployed in Kubernetes.

```
yaml
```

```yaml
apiVersion: apps/v1
kind: Deployment
metadata:
  name: nodejs-app-deployment
spec:
  replicas: 3
  selector:
    matchLabels:
      app: nodejs-app
```

185

```
template:
  metadata:
    labels:
      app: nodejs-app
  spec:
    containers:
    - name: nodejs-app
      image:        your-username/nodejs-
app:latest
      ports:
      - containerPort: 3000
```

Explanation:

- o **replicas**: **3**: Defines 3 instances (pods) of your Node.js app.
- o **image**: Specifies the Docker image for the app.
- o **containerPort**: Exposes port 3000 inside the container.
- **Service YAML**: Create a file called `service.yaml` to expose your app inside the cluster.

```
yaml
```

```
apiVersion: v1
kind: Service
metadata:
  name: nodejs-app-service
spec:
```

```
selector:
  app: nodejs-app
ports:
  - protocol: TCP
    port: 80
    targetPort: 3000
type: LoadBalancer
```

Explanation:

- o **targetPort: 3000**: Maps traffic on port 80 to port 3000 inside the container.
- o **type: LoadBalancer**: Exposes the service outside the Kubernetes cluster (ideal for cloud providers).

5. Deploying the Application: Run the following commands to create the deployment and service in your Kubernetes cluster:

bash

```
kubectl apply -f deployment.yaml
kubectl apply -f service.yaml
```

You can verify the deployment with:

bash

```
kubectl get pods
```

To check the service:

```
bash

kubectl get services
```

6. Accessing the Application:

- If using **Minikube**, you can access the service with:

```
bash

minikube service nodejs-app-service
```

- In a cloud environment (e.g., AWS), Kubernetes will automatically provision a load balancer for your service.

Scaling and Managing Microservices with Kubernetes

1. **Scaling the Application**: Kubernetes allows you to scale applications easily. To scale the Node.js application, use the following command:

```
bash

kubectl   scale   deployment   nodejs-app-
deployment --replicas=5
```

This command will increase the number of instances (pods) running your Node.js app to 5.

188

2. **Auto-Scaling with Kubernetes**: Kubernetes can also automatically scale services based on CPU usage or other metrics. To set up horizontal pod autoscaling, use the following command:

```bash
kubectl autoscale deployment nodejs-app-deployment --cpu-percent=50 --min=1 --max=10
```

This will scale the deployment between 1 and 10 replicas, depending on the CPU usage.

Real-World Example: Deploying Microservices on AWS Using Kubernetes

Deploying microservices on the cloud, such as **AWS**, requires using a cloud-managed Kubernetes service like **Amazon EKS** (Elastic Kubernetes Service). Let's walk through deploying a Node.js-based microservice on AWS using **EKS**.

1. Set Up EKS:

- **Create an EKS Cluster**: Use the AWS Management Console or AWS CLI to create an EKS cluster. You'll need to configure **kubectl** to interact with the cluster.

189

- **Configure IAM Roles**: Ensure the necessary IAM roles are set up for EKS to interact with other AWS services (e.g., EC2, IAM, VPC).

2. Set Up ECR (Elastic Container Registry):

- **Push Docker Images to ECR**: Push your Docker images to **AWS ECR** instead of Docker Hub. This allows EKS to pull the images from a secure, AWS-managed registry.

3. Deploying on EKS:

- Once your EKS cluster is set up, use `kubectl` to apply the Kubernetes deployment and service configurations (like `deployment.yaml` and `service.yaml`).

4. Exposing Services:

- Use **AWS Load Balancer** integration to expose the services and ensure high availability. Kubernetes automatically handles the integration with the AWS load balancer.

5. Managing Microservices in AWS:

- **Scaling**: Use Kubernetes Horizontal Pod Autoscaler (HPA) for automatic scaling based on load.

- **Monitoring**: Use AWS CloudWatch or Prometheus/Grafana for monitoring the health and performance of microservices.

Conclusion

In this chapter, we explored the role of **Kubernetes** in orchestrating microservices. Kubernetes helps manage the deployment, scaling, and monitoring of microservices in a cloud-native environment. We covered how to set up Kubernetes clusters for Node.js applications, scale and manage microservices with Kubernetes, and deploy microservices on **AWS** using **Amazon EKS**. Kubernetes provides powerful tools to ensure high availability, resource optimization, and easy scaling of your microservices architecture. By leveraging Kubernetes, you can efficiently manage complex microservices environments and ensure that your applications scale seamlessly with traffic demand.

CHAPTER 17

SECURING MICROSERVICES IN NODE.JS

In a microservices architecture, security is of paramount importance due to the distributed nature of the system. Each service in the architecture needs to be protected from potential attacks, such as Cross-Site Scripting (XSS), Cross-Site Request Forgery (CSRF), and SQL injection, which can exploit vulnerabilities in your services. Additionally, ensuring secure communication between services and protecting sensitive data are crucial for maintaining confidentiality, integrity, and availability. In this chapter, we will explore common security risks in microservices, how to use HTTPS and TLS for secure communication, how to protect sensitive data, and best practices for securing service-to-service communication.

Common Security Risks in Microservices

Microservices architecture introduces several unique security risks, primarily because services are often exposed to the internet and communicate with each other over networks. Here are some of the most common security risks in microservices:

1. **Cross-Site Scripting (XSS):**

o **Description**: XSS is a type of security vulnerability where malicious scripts are injected into a web page, allowing an attacker to execute arbitrary JavaScript in the browser of an unsuspecting user.

o **Impact**: This can lead to stealing session cookies, redirecting users to malicious sites, or executing malicious actions on behalf of the user.

o **Mitigation**: Use **input validation** and **output encoding** to prevent user inputs from being executed as code. Libraries like **Helmet.js** (for Node.js) can help secure your application by setting HTTP headers that prevent XSS attacks.

2. **Cross-Site Request Forgery (CSRF)**:

o **Description**: CSRF attacks trick users into performing actions on a web application where they are already authenticated. The attacker can send a request on behalf of the user, performing actions such as transferring funds or changing account settings.

o **Impact**: CSRF can compromise sensitive user actions, allowing attackers to exploit users' authenticated sessions.

o **Mitigation**: Protect your services by using anti-CSRF tokens (e.g., **csrf** package in Node.js). Additionally, ensure that state-changing requests use **HTTP POST** methods and check for valid tokens in request headers.

3. **SQL Injection**:

   o **Description**: SQL injection is a code injection technique where an attacker exploits vulnerabilities in an application's SQL query by inserting or manipulating SQL code through input fields.

   o **Impact**: It can result in unauthorized access to or manipulation of the database, leading to data breaches or corruption.

   o **Mitigation**: Always use **parameterized queries** (e.g., with **Sequelize** or **MongoDB**'s query mechanisms), and **validate** and **sanitize** user inputs to prevent malicious SQL code from being executed.

Using HTTPS and TLS for Secure Communication

One of the most effective ways to secure communication between microservices is by using **HTTPS** (HTTP Secure), which encrypts data using **TLS** (Transport Layer Security). TLS ensures that data transmitted between services is encrypted, protecting it from eavesdropping and tampering.

1. **Why Use HTTPS and TLS?**:

- o **Data Encryption**: TLS encrypts the data transmitted between microservices, ensuring that sensitive information is not exposed to unauthorized parties.
- o **Data Integrity**: TLS ensures that the data cannot be altered during transmission.
- o **Authentication**: With TLS, the identity of the service is verified using SSL certificates, ensuring that the communication is only happening with trusted services.

2. **Setting Up HTTPS in Node.js**: To set up HTTPS in a Node.js application, you need an SSL/TLS certificate. You can either use a self-signed certificate for testing or obtain a certificate from a trusted certificate authority (CA) for production.

- o **Generating a Self-Signed Certificate**: You can generate a self-signed certificate for testing purposes using OpenSSL:

```bash
openssl genpkey -algorithm RSA -out private-key.pem
openssl req -new -key private-key.pem -out csr.pem
openssl x509 -req -in csr.pem -signkey private-key.pem -out cert.pem
```

o **Setting Up HTTPS in Node.js**: With the certificate files (`cert.pem` and `private-key.pem`), you can set up HTTPS in your Node.js app.

javascript

```javascript
const https = require('https');
const fs = require('fs');
const express = require('express');

const app = express();

// Read the SSL certificate and
private key
const options = {
  cert: fs.readFileSync('cert.pem'),
  key:     fs.readFileSync('private-key.pem'),
};

// Define a simple route
app.get('/', (req, res) => {
  res.send('Hello, secure world!');
});

// Create an HTTPS server
https.createServer(options,
app).listen(3000, () => {
```

```
console.log('Secure app running on
https://localhost:3000');
});
```

3. **Important Notes**:
   o In production, it's recommended to use certificates from a trusted CA like **Let's Encrypt**.
   o Redirect all HTTP traffic to HTTPS to ensure secure communication.

4. **Service-to-Service Secure Communication**:
   o In a microservices architecture, internal communication between services should also be secured using HTTPS. You can configure your service discovery tool (like **Kubernetes**, **Consul**, or **Eureka**) to enforce HTTPS for internal communication.
   o Use mutual TLS (mTLS) to ensure that both the client and server authenticate each other before communication begins.

Protecting Sensitive Data and Service-to-Service Security

1. **Sensitive Data Protection**:
   o **Encryption at Rest**: Store sensitive data (e.g., passwords, API keys) in encrypted form, either in a database or a secure store. Use libraries like **bcrypt** to hash passwords before storing them.

197

- o **Environment Variables**: Store sensitive keys and secrets in environment variables, not in source code. Use tools like **dotenv** for managing environment variables.
- o **Data Masking**: Mask sensitive data like credit card numbers or social security numbers when displaying it to users. For example, only show the last 4 digits of a credit card number.

2. **Service-to-Service Security**: When microservices communicate with each other, especially in an internal network, ensuring the security of these communications is crucial.

- o **API Gateway**: Use an API Gateway (e.g., **Kong, Nginx, AWS API Gateway**) to act as a reverse proxy for handling authentication, authorization, and SSL termination. It can enforce security policies across all microservices.
- o **OAuth 2.0 and OpenID Connect**: Use **OAuth 2.0** and **OpenID Connect** for handling authentication and authorization across services. OAuth 2.0 allows your services to securely access resources on behalf of users, and OpenID Connect provides a framework for identity authentication.
- o **JWT (JSON Web Tokens)**: Use JWT tokens for secure service-to-service communication. When

one service makes a request to another, it includes a signed JWT that verifies its identity. The receiving service can validate the token using a public key.

Real-World Example: Securing Communication Between Microservices

Let's walk through an example of securing communication between two microservices: **Order Service** and **Payment Service**.

1. **Use Case**: The **Order Service** needs to call the **Payment Service** to process a payment when an order is created. Both services should communicate over HTTPS to ensure secure data transmission.

2. **Set Up HTTPS for Both Services**: Follow the steps in the **Setting Up HTTPS in Node.js** section to enable secure communication in both services. Both services should have their own SSL certificates, or you can use mutual TLS (mTLS) to ensure that both services authenticate each other.

3. **Securing API Requests with JWT**: When the **Order Service** calls the **Payment Service**, it will include a JWT token in the request header. This token will authenticate the **Order Service** and ensure that the request is coming from a trusted service.

- **Order Service** generates a JWT token (signed with a private key) and sends it along with the payment request.

javascript

```javascript
const jwt = require('jsonwebtoken');

const token = jwt.sign({ service: 'order-service' }, 'private-key', { expiresIn: '1h' });

const response = await fetch('https://payment-service.local/process', {
  method: 'POST',
  headers: {
    'Authorization': `Bearer ${token}`,
    'Content-Type': 'application/json'
  },
  body: JSON.stringify(paymentData),
});
```

- **Payment Service** validates the JWT token to verify the identity of the **Order Service**.

javascript

```
const jwt = require('jsonwebtoken');

const token =
req.headers['authorization'].split(
' ')[1];    // Extract token from
header

try {
  const decoded = jwt.verify(token,
'public-key');
  if (decoded.service !== 'order-
service') {
    return
res.status(403).send('Forbidden');
  }
  // Proceed with payment processing
} catch (err) {
  return
res.status(401).send('Invalid
token');
}
```

4. **Note**: Both services should share a public/private key pair, with the **Order Service** using the private key to sign the JWT and the **Payment Service** using the public key to verify it.

5. **Ensure HTTPS Communication**: The **Payment Service** should enforce HTTPS for all incoming requests to ensure that data is encrypted during transmission.

Conclusion

In this chapter, we discussed essential techniques for securing microservices in a Node.js environment. We covered common security risks like **XSS**, **CSRF**, and **SQL injection** and explored how to mitigate these risks. We also learned how to use **HTTPS** and **TLS** to secure communication between microservices, ensuring encrypted data transmission. Additionally, we explored techniques for protecting sensitive data and implementing service-to-service security using **JWT**, **OAuth 2.0**, and **mTLS**. Finally, we demonstrated a real-world example of securing communication between the **Order Service** and the **Payment Service** using secure protocols and JWT for authentication. By applying these security practices, you can protect your microservices and ensure that data remains secure in transit and at rest.

CHAPTER 18

TESTING MICROSERVICES

Testing is a crucial part of ensuring the reliability, stability, and correctness of microservices. As microservices communicate with each other and handle business logic, it's important to test them at various levels, from unit testing individual functions to integration testing multiple services. In this chapter, we will explore the essentials of **testing microservices**, using tools like **Mocha** and **Chai** for unit testing, performing integration testing between services, and adopting **Continuous Testing** and **Test-Driven Development (TDD)**. Finally, we will walk through a real-world example of writing tests for a **user registration service.**

Unit Testing Microservices with Mocha and Chai

Unit testing focuses on testing individual components of a microservice, such as functions or methods, in isolation. The goal is to ensure that each unit of the service behaves as expected. In Node.js applications, **Mocha** is one of the most widely used testing frameworks, and **Chai** is an assertion library that makes it easy to write test assertions.

1. **Setting Up Mocha and Chai**: To get started, we need to install Mocha and Chai in our project:

```bash
npm install mocha chai --save-dev
```

2. **Writing Unit Tests**: Let's say we have a simple function in our **User Service** that validates the user's email address. We will write a unit test to ensure it works as expected.

    o   **Function to Test** (userService.js):

```javascript
function isValidEmail(email) {
  const regex = /^[a-zA-Z0-9._-]+@[a-zA-Z0-9.-]+\.[a-zA-Z]{2,6}$/;
  return regex.test(email);
}

module.exports = { isValidEmail };
```

    o   **Unit Test with Mocha and Chai** (test/userService.test.js):

```javascript
const chai = require('chai');
const expect = chai.expect;
const userService = require('../userService');
```

```
describe('User Service', function() {
  describe('isValidEmail', function() {
    it('should    return    true    for    valid
email', function() {
      const email = 'test@example.com';
      const           result           =
userService.isValidEmail(email);
      expect(result).to.be.true;
    });

    it('should    return    false    for    invalid
email', function() {
      const email = 'invalid-email';
      const           result           =
userService.isValidEmail(email);
      expect(result).to.be.false;
    });
  });
});
```

Explanation:

- We define a simple **isValidEmail** function in the userService.js file, which uses a regular expression to check the validity of an email.
- The test file uses **Mocha**'s describe and it functions to define test suites and test cases.

o **Chai's expect** is used to assert that the result of `isValidEmail` matches the expected value.

3. **Running the Tests**: Once the tests are written, you can run them using the Mocha command:

```bash

npx mocha test/userService.test.js
```

This will execute the test and show the results in the terminal.

Integration Testing Between Services

Integration testing ensures that different microservices or components of a system work together as expected. For example, when one service makes a request to another service, integration tests verify that the request-response cycle works correctly.

In microservices, integration testing typically involves:

- Setting up real or mock service endpoints.
- Testing how services communicate over HTTP (or other protocols).
- Validating the responses and ensuring correct data flow.

1. **Integration Test Example**: Let's consider the **User Service** interacting with a **Database Service**. The **User**

Service validates and registers a new user by calling the **Database Service** to store the user data.

- o **User Registration Integration Test** (`test/userRegistration.test.js`):

javascript

```javascript
const chai = require('chai');
const expect = chai.expect;
const request = require('supertest');
const app = require('../app'); // Express
app

describe('User    Registration    Service',
function() {
  it('should    register    a    new    user',
function(done) {
    const userData = {
      username: 'john_doe',
      email: 'john.doe@example.com',
      password: 'password123'
    };

    request(app)
      .post('/register')
      .send(userData)
      .expect(201)
      .end(function(err, res) {
        if (err) return done(err);
```

```
expect(res.body.message).to.equal('User
registered successfully');
        done();
      });
  });
});
```

Explanation:

- o The test uses **Supertest** (a popular testing library for HTTP assertions) to send a POST request to the /register route of the **User Service**.
- o The test validates that the response status is 201 (Created) and the response body contains the success message "User registered successfully".

2. **Mocking External Services**: In real-world integration testing, external dependencies like databases, external APIs, or third-party services should be mocked to ensure the tests are isolated. Tools like **Sinon.js** or **Nock** can be used to mock HTTP requests.

Continuous Testing and Test-Driven Development (TDD)

Continuous Testing and **Test-Driven Development (TDD)** are important practices that help ensure your code remains robust and reliable as you develop and deploy microservices.

1. **Continuous Testing**: Continuous testing involves running tests automatically every time you make a change to the codebase. This helps catch bugs early and ensures that new features don't break existing functionality.

   o **Tools** like **Jenkins, Travis CI**, or **GitHub Actions** can be set up to automatically run tests on every commit or pull request.

   o **Example**: Set up a **GitHub Actions workflow** to run your tests automatically on each commit.

   o **GitHub Actions Example** (`.github/workflows/test.yml`):

```yaml
name: Node.js CI

on:
  push:
    branches:
      - main

jobs:
  test:
    runs-on: ubuntu-latest

    steps:
      - name: Checkout code
        uses: actions/checkout@v2
```

```
- name: Set up Node.js
  uses: actions/setup-node@v2
  with:
      node-version: '14'

- name: Install dependencies
  run: npm install

- name: Run tests
  run: npm test
```

2. **Test-Driven Development (TDD)**: TDD is a software development approach where tests are written before the actual code. The workflow follows three steps:
   1. **Write a test** that defines the functionality you want to implement.
   2. **Write the minimum code** necessary to pass the test.
   3. **Refactor** the code and tests to improve them.

TDD helps ensure that the system is thoroughly tested from the start and encourages developers to write more modular, testable code.

Example: For a **User Registration Service**, you would:

o Write tests for user validation, email format validation, and password hashing before writing the implementation logic.

o Write just enough code to make the tests pass.

o Refactor the code for readability and efficiency.

Real-World Example: Writing Tests for the User Registration Service

Let's walk through how to write tests for the **User Registration Service** using Mocha, Chai, and Supertest.

1. **Set Up the User Registration Route** (`app.js`): Assume we have an Express-based **User Registration Service** that validates and registers users.

javascript

```
const express = require('express');
const app = express();
const bodyParser = require('body-parser');
const           UserService           =
require('./userService'); // Hypothetical
service

app.use(bodyParser.json());

app.post('/register', async (req, res) =>
{
```

```
const { username, email, password } =
req.body;
  try {
    const      user      =      await
UserService.registerUser(username,  email,
password);
    res.status(201).json({ message:  'User
registered successfully', user });
  } catch (error) {
    res.status(400).json({ message:  'User
registration failed', error });
  }
});

module.exports = app;
```

2. **Write   Tests   for   User   Registration**
   (test/userRegistration.test.js): Write tests to
   check the user registration flow and validation.

```
javascript
```

```
const chai = require('chai');
const expect = chai.expect;
const request = require('supertest');
const app = require('../app');

describe('User Registration', function() {
```

```
it('should    register    a    new    user
successfully', function(done) {
    const user = { username: 'testUser',
email:  'testuser@example.com',  password:
'password123' };

    request(app)
      .post('/register')
      .send(user)
      .expect(201)
      .end(function(err, res) {
        if (err) return done(err);

expect(res.body.message).to.equal('User
registered successfully');

expect(res.body.user.username).to.equal('
testUser');
        done();
      });
  });


it('should    return    400    if    email    is
invalid', function(done) {
    const user = { username: 'testUser',
email:      'invalid-email',      password:
'password123' };

    request(app)
```

213

```
        .post('/register')
        .send(user)
        .expect(400)
        .end(function(err, res) {
            if (err) return done(err);

expect(res.body.message).to.equal('User
registration failed');
            done();
        });
    });
});
```

Explanation:

- The first test case checks if a user is registered successfully and ensures the correct response is returned.
- The second test case checks if invalid email format is handled properly by the service.

Conclusion

In this chapter, we covered how to write **unit tests**, **integration tests**, and implement **continuous testing** for microservices. We used **Mocha** and **Chai** for unit testing and **Supertest** for integration testing HTTP APIs. We also explored the importance of **Test-Driven Development (TDD)** and discussed how to automate tests using CI/CD pipelines. Finally, we provided a real-world example of writing tests for a **User Registration Service**, which ensures that the service functions correctly and handles various edge cases. By incorporating thorough testing into your microservices development, you can ensure that your services are reliable, maintainable, and robust.

CHAPTER 19

DEPLOYING MICROSERVICES TO THE CLOUD

Cloud platforms have become the go-to choice for deploying microservices due to their scalability, reliability, and flexibility. In this chapter, we will explore how to deploy **Node.js microservices** to various cloud platforms such as **AWS, Azure**, and **Google Cloud**. We will also discuss the importance of **Continuous Integration and Continuous Deployment (CI/CD)** and how to automate deployments. Finally, we'll walk through a real-world example of automating deployments using **Jenkins**.

Deploying Node.js Microservices to Cloud Platforms

The process of deploying microservices to the cloud involves several steps: selecting a cloud platform, configuring the environment, deploying your services, and managing resources. The most commonly used cloud platforms for deploying microservices are **AWS, Azure**, and **Google Cloud**. Let's take a look at how to deploy Node.js microservices to each of these platforms.

1. Deploying Node.js Microservices on AWS

AWS (Amazon Web Services) offers a wide range of tools to deploy and manage microservices, including **Elastic Beanstalk**, **ECS (Elastic Container Service)**, and **EKS (Elastic Kubernetes Service)**.

- **Elastic Beanstalk**: AWS Elastic Beanstalk is an easy-to-use service for deploying and managing applications. It automatically handles the deployment, from provisioning resources to load balancing and auto-scaling.

Steps to Deploy a Node.js Application to AWS Elastic Beanstalk:

1. **Install the AWS CLI**: If you don't already have it, install the AWS Command Line Interface (CLI) to interact with AWS services.
2. **Prepare the Application**: Make sure your Node.js application is ready for deployment, with a proper `package.json` file and other necessary files.
3. **Create an Elastic Beanstalk Application**:
    - Run the following command to initialize Elastic Beanstalk:

    bash

    ```
    eb init
    ```

Follow the prompts to select the appropriate region and platform (Node.js).

4. **Deploy the Application**:
   o Run the following command to deploy your Node.js application:

```bash

eb create my-nodejs-app
```

   o After the environment is created, use this command to deploy updates:

```bash

eb deploy
```

5. **Access Your Application**:
   o After deployment, you can access your app using the URL provided by Elastic Beanstalk.

---

2. Deploying Node.js Microservices on Azure

Azure offers **App Service** for managing and deploying Node.js applications, as well as **Azure Kubernetes Service (AKS)** for containerized applications.

Steps to Deploy a Node.js Application to Azure App Service:

1. **Install Azure CLI**: Install the Azure CLI to manage Azure resources from your local machine.

2. **Create an Azure Web App**:
   - Log in to your Azure account:

   ```bash

   az login
   ```

   - Create a new resource group:

   ```bash

   az group create --name myResourceGroup --location eastus
   ```

   - Create an App Service Plan:

   ```bash

   az appservice plan create --name myAppServicePlan --resource-group myResourceGroup --sku B1 --is-linux
   ```

   - Create a web app:

   ```bash
   ```

```
az  webapp  create  --resource-group
myResourceGroup            --plan
myAppServicePlan  --name  my-nodejs-
app --runtime "NODE|14-lts"
```

3. **Deploy the Application**:
   - o You can deploy the Node.js app via **Git**, **FTP**, or using the **Azure CLI**.
   - o Use the following command to deploy via Git:

   ```bash
   ```

   ```
   git push azure master
   ```

4. **Access Your Application**:
   - o Once deployed, your application will be accessible via the URL provided by Azure (e.g., `https://my-nodejs-app.azurewebsites.net`).

---

3. Deploying Node.js Microservices on Google Cloud

Google Cloud offers services like **Google Kubernetes Engine (GKE)**, **App Engine**, and **Cloud Run** for deploying containerized applications and microservices.

Steps to Deploy a Node.js Application to Google Cloud App Engine:

1. **Install Google Cloud SDK**: Install the Google Cloud SDK to interact with Google Cloud resources.

2. **Prepare the Application**: Ensure your Node.js application has an `app.yaml` file, which is required for deploying to App Engine.

   Example `app.yaml`:

   ```yaml
   runtime: nodejs14

   env_variables:
     NODE_ENV: 'production'

   instance_class: F2
   ```

3. **Deploy the Application**:
   - o Navigate to the project folder and run the following command to deploy:

   ```bash
   gcloud app deploy
   ```

4. **Access Your Application**:

221

o After deployment, your app will be available at the URL provided by Google Cloud (e.g., `https://your-app-id.appspot.com`).

Continuous Integration and Continuous Deployment (CI/CD) Pipelines

CI/CD is a set of practices and tools used to automate the process of integrating code changes into a shared repository (CI) and deploying them to production (CD). CI/CD pipelines are essential in microservices architectures to ensure that updates are deployed quickly and reliably.

1. **Continuous Integration (CI)**:
   o **CI tools**: Jenkins, Travis CI, CircleCI, GitLab CI, and GitHub Actions are commonly used for CI.
   o **Process**: Developers commit code to a version control system (like Git). The CI tool automatically runs tests and checks for errors.

2. **Continuous Deployment (CD)**:
   o **CD tools**: Jenkins, Spinnaker, and Argo CD help automate the deployment process.
   o **Process**: Once the code passes tests, it is automatically deployed to production or staging environments.

Real-World Example: Automating Deployments with Jenkins

Jenkins is one of the most popular tools for automating builds and deployments. It integrates well with version control systems like Git and allows you to automate testing and deployment pipelines.

1. **Install Jenkins**: Follow the instructions to install Jenkins on your system or use a **Jenkins-as-a-Service** option (e.g., **Jenkins Cloud**).

2. **Create a New Jenkins Job**:
   - Open the Jenkins dashboard and click on **New Item**.
   - Select **Freestyle project** and give it a name (e.g., "Node.js Microservice CI/CD").
   - Under **Source Code Management**, connect your Git repository (e.g., GitHub).

3. **Set Up Build Triggers**:
   - Set Jenkins to trigger a build whenever changes are pushed to the repository (using **GitHub webhook** or **poll SCM**).

4. **Define Build Steps**:
   - Add build steps to install dependencies, run tests, and build the Docker image:

```bash
bash

npm install
npm test
docker build -t nodejs-app .
```

5. **Deploy to Cloud**:
   - o After building the image, add a step to deploy it to the cloud (e.g., Elastic Beanstalk, App Engine, or Kubernetes):

```bash
bash

eb deploy  # For AWS Elastic Beanstalk
gcloud app deploy  # For Google Cloud App Engine
```

6. **Set Up Notifications**:
   - o Configure Jenkins to send email or Slack notifications on build success or failure.

Conclusion

In this chapter, we explored how to deploy **Node.js microservices** to popular cloud platforms, including **AWS**, **Azure**, and **Google Cloud**. We covered the steps for deploying to **Elastic Beanstalk**, **Azure App Service**, and **Google Cloud App Engine**.

Additionally, we discussed **Continuous Integration and Continuous Deployment (CI/CD)** pipelines, which automate the process of testing and deploying code, ensuring that microservices are deployed quickly and reliably. Lastly, we provided a **real-world example** of automating deployments with **Jenkins**, demonstrating how to integrate testing and deployment in a CI/CD pipeline.

By using cloud platforms and CI/CD tools, you can automate the deployment process, ensuring that your microservices remain scalable, secure, and always up-to-date. These practices also reduce manual errors, improve collaboration between teams, and accelerate the delivery of new features and updates.

CHAPTER 20

MONITORING AND MAINTAINING MICROSERVICES

As microservices architectures grow, monitoring and maintaining the health of these distributed services becomes essential. With microservices running across different environments, it's crucial to ensure that each service is operating correctly, that performance is optimized, and that any issues are identified and addressed quickly. In this chapter, we will discuss the importance of monitoring microservices, explore popular monitoring tools like **Prometheus**, **Grafana**, and the **ELK stack**, and look at how to set up health checks and alerts. Finally, we will walk through a real-world example of setting up a health check endpoint for your microservices.

Importance of Monitoring Microservices

Monitoring is crucial for maintaining the availability, performance, and reliability of microservices. Without proper monitoring, it's difficult to track the behavior of your services, identify bottlenecks, or diagnose failures. Monitoring also helps ensure that microservices are performing as expected in real-time and that any disruptions are quickly detected.

Key benefits of monitoring microservices include:

1. **Improved Availability and Reliability**:
   - Monitoring helps detect service failures early, allowing for quick intervention. With microservices often deployed across multiple servers or containers, continuous monitoring ensures that individual service failures don't affect the entire system.

2. **Performance Optimization**:
   - By tracking response times, resource usage (CPU, memory), and latency, monitoring can help identify performance bottlenecks. This allows you to optimize the services for better performance.

3. **Troubleshooting and Debugging**:
   - When issues arise, monitoring helps trace back the problem to specific services or dependencies. Logs and metrics give detailed insights into the root cause of failures.

4. **Scaling Decisions**:
   - Monitoring data can provide insights into the load on your microservices, helping you decide when to scale services up or down based on demand.

5. **Security Monitoring**:

o Monitoring helps detect unauthorized access, abnormal traffic patterns, or other potential security threats in real-time.

Tools for Monitoring: Prometheus, Grafana, and ELK Stack

To effectively monitor microservices, several tools can be integrated to collect and visualize metrics, logs, and health status. Here's an overview of some of the most popular tools for monitoring microservices.

1. Prometheus

Prometheus is an open-source monitoring and alerting toolkit designed for reliability and scalability. It collects metrics from configured targets at specified intervals, stores them, and allows you to query the data using its powerful query language (PromQL).

Key Features of Prometheus:

- **Metrics Collection**: Prometheus collects and stores time-series data (e.g., request counts, error rates, latency).
- **Alerting**: Prometheus supports alerting rules that trigger notifications based on thresholds.
- **Service Discovery**: It can automatically discover and scrape metrics from microservices running in

environments like Kubernetes, Docker, or cloud platforms.

Setting Up Prometheus for Node.js:

1. **Install Prometheus**: Follow the Prometheus installation guide for your environment.
2. **Expose Metrics from Node.js Microservices**: You can expose application metrics in Prometheus format by using the `prom-client` library for Node.js.

   o   Install `prom-client`:

   ```bash
   npm install prom-client
   ```

   o   Add Prometheus metrics to your Node.js app:

   ```javascript
   const express = require('express');
   const promClient = require('prom-client');
   const app = express();

   const register = new promClient.Registry();
   promClient.collectDefaultMetrics({ register });
   ```

```
// Create a custom metric for
tracking HTTP requests
const httpRequestsTotal = new
promClient.Counter({
  name: 'http_requests_total',
  help: 'Total number of HTTP
requests',
  labelNames: ['method', 'status'],
});

app.use((req, res, next) => {
  res.on('finish', () => {
    httpRequestsTotal.inc({ method:
req.method, status: res.statusCode
});
  });
  next();
});

// Expose metrics on a /metrics
endpoint
app.get('/metrics', (req, res) => {
  res.set('Content-Type',
register.contentType);
  res.end(await register.metrics());
});

app.listen(3000, () => {
```

```
console.log('App    is    running    on
http://localhost:3000');
});
```

3. In this example, we set up a custom counter (`http_requests_total`) that tracks the number of HTTP requests, categorized by the method (GET, POST) and the status code (200, 404).

2. Grafana

Grafana is an open-source data visualization and monitoring tool that integrates with various data sources like Prometheus, InfluxDB, and Elasticsearch. It provides interactive and visually appealing dashboards that display real-time metrics.

Key Features of Grafana:

- **Real-Time Dashboards**: Grafana allows you to visualize the health and performance metrics of your microservices in real-time.
- **Alerts**: Set up alerts on your dashboards to notify you when thresholds are exceeded (e.g., high error rates, response times).
- **Data Sources**: Grafana integrates with Prometheus to pull metrics and visualize them.

Setting Up Grafana with Prometheus:

1. **Install Grafana**: Follow the Grafana installation guide.
2. **Connect Grafana to Prometheus**:
   o Open Grafana and go to the "Data Sources" section in the settings.
   o Select **Prometheus** as the data source and enter the Prometheus server URL (e.g., `http://localhost:9090`).
3. **Create Dashboards**:
   o Once the data source is set up, create a new dashboard to visualize the metrics, such as HTTP request counts, error rates, and response times.

3. ELK Stack (Elasticsearch, Logstash, and Kibana)

The **ELK stack** is a powerful combination of tools used for logging and monitoring:

- **Elasticsearch**: A search and analytics engine that stores logs and allows for querying and aggregating data.
- **Logstash**: A data processing pipeline that collects, transforms, and sends logs to Elasticsearch.
- **Kibana**: A data visualization tool that works with Elasticsearch to create interactive dashboards for logs.

Key Features of the ELK Stack:

- **Centralized Logging**: Aggregate logs from all microservices in one place for easy searching and troubleshooting.
- **Real-Time Insights**: Visualize logs and system metrics in real-time through Kibana dashboards.
- **Full-Text Search**: Elasticsearch allows you to search logs with advanced filtering and querying.

Setting Up ELK Stack for Node.js:

1. **Install Elasticsearch and Kibana**:
   - o Follow the Elasticsearch installation guide.
   - o Follow the Kibana installation guide.
2. **Send Logs from Node.js to Elasticsearch**:
   - o Use **Winston** or **Bunyan** for logging in your Node.js app. Here's an example using **Winston**:

```javascript
const winston = require('winston');
require('winston-elasticsearch');

const esTransportOptions = {
  level: 'info',
  clientOpts: {
    node: 'http://localhost:9200',
  },
};
```

```
const               logger               =
winston.createLogger({
  transports: [
    new
winston.transports.Console(),
    new
winston.transports.Elasticsearch(es
TransportOptions),
  ],
});

logger.info('This    is    an    info
message');
logger.error('This   is   an   error
message');
```

o In this example, logs are sent to Elasticsearch, where they can be indexed and visualized in Kibana.

Setting Up Health Checks and Alerts

1. **Health Checks**: A **health check endpoint** is a simple endpoint that external systems or monitoring tools can query to determine if your microservice is running properly.

- o **Node.js Example**: You can create a `/health` route that returns a `200 OK` status if the service is healthy:

```javascript
app.get('/health', (req, res) => {
  res.status(200).json({     status:
'Service is up and running' });
});
```

- o **Kubernetes Health Checks**: If you are deploying microservices in Kubernetes, you can configure **liveness** and **readiness probes** to automatically monitor the health of your containers.

  Example Kubernetes configuration for a health check:

```yaml
apiVersion: apps/v1
kind: Deployment
metadata:
  name: nodejs-app
spec:
  containers:
    - name: nodejs-app
```

```
image: nodejs-app:latest
ports:
  - containerPort: 3000
livenessProbe:
  httpGet:
    path: /health
    port: 3000
  initialDelaySeconds: 3
  periodSeconds: 5
readinessProbe:
  httpGet:
    path: /health
    port: 3000
  initialDelaySeconds: 5
  periodSeconds: 5
```

2. **Alerts**: Setting up alerts allows you to be notified when certain thresholds are breached (e.g., high CPU usage, memory consumption, or increased error rates). You can set up alerts in Prometheus or Grafana.

   o **Prometheus Alerts**: You can define alert rules in Prometheus. For example, if the error rate exceeds a certain threshold, Prometheus can send an alert:

   yaml

   ```
   groups:
     - name: example
   ```

```
rules:
  - alert: HighErrorRate
    expr:
http_requests_total{status="500"}  >
100
    for: 5m
    labels:
      severity: critical
    annotations:
      summary: "High error rate
detected"
```

o **Grafana Alerts**: Grafana allows you to create alerts on visualized metrics. You can define alert thresholds in the dashboard settings and configure notifications (e.g., email, Slack).

Real-World Example: Setting Up a Health Check Endpoint for Microservices

Let's implement a **health check** for a Node.js-based **User Service**.

1. **Create the Health Check Endpoint**:

   In the userService.js file, add a /health endpoint:

   ```
   javascript
   ```

```javascript
const express = require('express');
const app = express();

app.get('/health', (req, res) => {
  res.status(200).json({ status: 'User
Service is running' });
});

app.listen(3000, () => {
  console.log('User Service is running on
port 3000');
});
```

2. **Configure Prometheus**: Expose the /metrics endpoint for Prometheus to scrape:

javascript

```
const promClient = require('prom-client');
const register = new
promClient.Registry();
promClient.collectDefaultMetrics({
register });

app.get('/metrics', async (req, res) => {
  res.set('Content-Type',
register.contentType);
  res.end(await register.metrics());
});
```

3. **Set Up Grafana Dashboard**:

   o Create a dashboard to visualize metrics such as response times, error rates, and the health of the service.

   o Set up alerts for failures or high error rates in the User Service.

Conclusion

In this chapter, we discussed the importance of monitoring and maintaining microservices to ensure that they are running efficiently and reliably. We explored popular tools like **Prometheus**, **Grafana**, and the **ELK stack** for monitoring microservices, as well as how to set up health checks and alerts to proactively identify issues. Finally, we provided a real-world example of setting up a health check endpoint for the **User Service**, demonstrating how to expose metrics for monitoring. Effective monitoring and maintenance practices help ensure the stability, scalability, and performance of microservices in production environments.

CHAPTER 21

MANAGING CONFIGURATION AND SECRETS

In a microservices architecture, managing configuration and secrets securely is crucial. Microservices often require access to various configurations (such as API keys, database credentials, and service URLs) that need to be stored safely and securely. Improper management of these configurations can lead to security vulnerabilities and operational issues. In this chapter, we will discuss how to store configuration in microservices, use **environment variables** for sensitive data, leverage tools like **Vault** for managing secrets, and provide a real-world example of configuring a payment gateway API securely.

Storing Configuration in Microservices

Configuration management is essential in microservices because each service might have its own specific configuration needs, such as environment-specific settings, external service credentials, and feature toggles. There are several ways to handle configurations in microservices:

1. **Configuration Files**:

240

o Configuration files (like JSON, YAML, or properties files) can be used to store settings. However, managing configurations in files might be cumbersome as the number of services increases. Additionally, storing sensitive information such as passwords or API keys in these files could lead to security risks.

2. **Environment Variables**:

o The most common and secure method for managing configuration is to store them in **environment variables**. This allows you to separate configuration from the code and securely store sensitive data like API keys, database credentials, and other secret values.

o For example, you can define environment variables like:

```bash
DB_HOST=localhost
DB_USER=username
DB_PASSWORD=password
```

These values can then be accessed inside your microservices through the `process.env` object in Node.js:

```
javascript
```

241

```
const dbHost = process.env.DB_HOST;
const dbUser = process.env.DB_USER;
const         dbPassword        =
process.env.DB_PASSWORD;
```

3. **Centralized Configuration Management**:
   - For large-scale microservices systems, you may need a centralized configuration management system that can manage configurations for all microservices. Tools like **Spring Cloud Config** (for Java-based services), **Consul**, and **etcd** can be used for centralizing configurations.

Using Environment Variables for Sensitive Data

Sensitive data, such as API keys, authentication tokens, and database passwords, should never be hard-coded in the source code or configuration files. Instead, these values should be stored in environment variables, which can be injected into the application at runtime. This approach minimizes the risk of exposing sensitive data, especially in version control systems.

1. **Environment Variables in Development**:
   - In local development environments, you can use **dotenv** to load environment variables from a .env file into process.env in Node.js.

- Install **dotenv**:

```bash
npm install dotenv
```

- Create a .env file to store sensitive data:

```bash
DB_HOST=localhost
DB_USER=myuser
DB_PASSWORD=mypassword
```

- In your application code, load the environment variables:

```javascript
require('dotenv').config();

const         dbHost        =
process.env.DB_HOST;
const         dbUser        =
process.env.DB_USER;
const       dbPassword      =
process.env.DB_PASSWORD;
```

2. **Environment Variables in Production**:

243

- o For production environments, you can set environment variables directly on the hosting platform (e.g., AWS, Azure, Heroku) or use Docker to pass them during container creation.

- o **Docker Example**: To pass environment variables to a Docker container, you can use the -e flag:

bash

```
docker     run     -e     DB_HOST=prod-
db.example.com  -e  DB_USER=prod-user
-e   DB_PASSWORD=prod-password   my-
nodejs-app
```

3. **Best Practices**:

- o Never store sensitive data in your source code or commit it to version control systems.

- o Use tools like **Docker Secrets**, **Kubernetes Secrets**, or **AWS Secrets Manager** to securely manage environment variables in production.

Tools Like Vault for Managing Secrets

Vault is a popular open-source tool developed by HashiCorp for managing secrets securely. It provides a centralized solution for securely storing and accessing secrets, such as API keys, passwords, certificates, and database credentials.

Key Features of Vault:

1. **Dynamic Secrets**: Vault can generate secrets dynamically for services like databases, AWS, or cloud providers, providing one-time credentials that are valid for a specific session or a short duration.
2. **Encryption as a Service**: Vault can encrypt and decrypt sensitive data using its own encryption keys, without exposing the raw data.
3. **Access Control**: Vault provides fine-grained access control policies, allowing only authorized services or users to access certain secrets.
4. **Audit Logging**: Vault logs all access requests, providing an audit trail for security compliance.

Setting Up Vault for Managing Secrets:

1. **Install Vault**:
   o Follow the installation instructions on the HashiCorp Vault website for your platform.
2. **Start Vault**: You can run Vault in development mode for testing:

```bash
vault server -dev
```

3. **Store a Secret**: Once Vault is running, you can store a secret (e.g., an API key):

bash

```
vault kv put secret/payment-gateway/api-
key value="your-api-key-here"
```

4. **Access a Secret**: To retrieve the secret in your application, you would authenticate to Vault and read the secret:

bash

```
const axios = require('axios');

// Example of retrieving secret from Vault
(assuming Vault is unsealed and running)
const         response      =       await
axios.get('http://127.0.0.1:8200/v1/secre
t/data/payment-gateway/api-key', {
  headers: { 'X-Vault-Token': 'your-vault-
token' }
});
const apiKey = response.data.data.value;
```

5. **Integrating Vault with Kubernetes**:

    o   If you're running microservices in **Kubernetes**, Vault integrates seamlessly with Kubernetes to manage secrets securely.

Benefits of Using Vault:

- Centralized management of secrets across your services.
- Dynamic secrets to reduce the risk of long-lived credentials.
- Auditing capabilities to track access to sensitive data.
- Integration with various systems and platforms.

Real-World Example: Configuring a Payment Gateway API Securely

Let's walk through an example of configuring a **Payment Gateway API** securely in a Node.js-based microservice. The goal is to securely store the **API key** for the payment gateway and ensure that it's not hard-coded in the source code.

1. **Step 1: Store the Payment Gateway API Key in Vault**
   - Store the API key for the payment gateway in Vault as a secret:

```bash
```

```
vault     kv     put    secret/payment-
gateway/api-key value="your-payment-
gateway-api-key"
```

2. **Step 2: Retrieve the API Key in the User Service**

In your **User Service**, you need to securely fetch the payment gateway API key from Vault to make API calls.

   o   **Install Axios** (for making HTTP requests) and **dotenv** (for loading environment variables):

   bash

   ```
   npm install axios dotenv
   ```

   o   Create a .env file to store the Vault server URL and Vault token (in a production environment, this token should be securely passed through environment variables):

   bash

   ```
   VAULT_ADDR=http://127.0.0.1:8200
   VAULT_TOKEN=your-vault-token
   ```

   o   In your Node.js code, load the Vault address and token, and retrieve the payment gateway API key securely:

```javascript

require('dotenv').config();
const axios = require('axios');

const vaultAddr = process.env.VAULT_ADDR;
const vaultToken = process.env.VAULT_TOKEN;

async function getPaymentGatewayApiKey() {
  try {
    const response = await axios.get(`${vaultAddr}/v1/secret/data/payment-gateway/api-key`, {
      headers: { 'X-Vault-Token': vaultToken }
    });
    return response.data.data.value;
  } catch (error) {
    console.error('Error retrieving API key:', error);
    return null;
  }
}

async function processPayment(orderDetails) {
```

```
const       apiKey    =       await
getPaymentGatewayApiKey();
  if (!apiKey) {
    throw  new  Error('Failed  to
retrieve API key');
  }

  // Use  the  API  key  to  make  a
payment request
  const  paymentResponse  =  await
axios.post('https://payment-
gateway.com/api/pay', {
    apiKey,
    orderDetails,
  });

  // Process payment response
  console.log('Payment    response:',
paymentResponse.data);
}
```

3. **Step 3: Configure Vault Access Control and Audit Logging**

    o **Vault Policies**: Create a Vault policy to allow only the necessary services to access the payment gateway secrets.

    o **Audit Logging**: Enable audit logging in Vault to track access to the secrets for compliance purposes.

Conclusion

In this chapter, we covered essential techniques for **managing configuration and secrets** securely in microservices. We discussed the importance of using **environment variables** for sensitive data and explored tools like **Vault** for securely managing secrets. We also walked through a real-world example of configuring a **payment gateway API** securely in a Node.js microservice by storing the API key in Vault and retrieving it at runtime. By using these best practices, you can ensure that sensitive information in your microservices is protected and that configurations are managed efficiently and securely.

CHAPTER 22

MICROSERVICES TESTING AT SCALE

As microservices architectures grow in complexity, testing them at scale presents unique challenges. Microservices often operate in distributed environments, communicate over networks, and depend on other services, making testing more difficult. To ensure the reliability and performance of microservices at scale, we need robust testing strategies that cover not only functionality but also performance and resilience under heavy load. In this chapter, we will explore the challenges of testing microservices at scale, discuss end-to-end testing with tools like **Postman**, and look at how to simulate high traffic and perform load testing. Finally, we will walk through a real-world example of **stress-testing a product catalog microservice**.

Challenges of Testing Microservices at Scale

Testing microservices at scale comes with several unique challenges:

1. **Service Dependencies**:

o   Microservices often interact with other services, databases, message queues, and third-party APIs. Ensuring that all dependencies are accounted for in tests can be difficult, especially when testing in a production-like environment.

2. **Distributed Systems**:

    o   Unlike monolithic applications, microservices are distributed across different machines or containers, which adds complexity to testing. Communication failures, network latency, and inconsistencies between services can complicate test results.

3. **Complex Test Environments**:

    o   Setting up test environments that replicate the real-world production environment can be time-consuming and expensive. It's challenging to simulate all the services, databases, and networks that a microservices-based system depends on.

4. **Data Management**:

    o   Microservices often require access to various types of data (e.g., user data, transaction data). Ensuring consistency across microservices when testing different environments (e.g., testing with real data vs. mock data) can lead to potential issues.

5. **Fault Tolerance and Resilience**:

o   Microservices must be resilient to failures in other services or networks. Simulating failure scenarios (e.g., network partitioning, service crashes) during testing is essential to ensure that the system behaves correctly under stress.

6. **Scaling and Performance**:

o   As the number of microservices increases, it becomes harder to test the entire system's performance, scalability, and capacity. Simulating high traffic and load testing is crucial to identify bottlenecks and ensure the system can scale.

End-to-End Testing with Tools Like Postman

End-to-end testing involves testing the entire workflow of a microservices system, from the user interface to the backend services, to ensure that all components are working together as expected.

Postman is one of the most widely used tools for testing APIs and microservices. It allows you to create, test, and automate API requests, making it ideal for testing microservices in an isolated or integrated manner.

1. **Setting Up Postman for Testing Microservices**:

- o **Create Collections**: In Postman, you can organize your API tests into collections. Each collection can contain multiple requests that simulate interactions with different microservices.

- o **Environment Variables**: Postman supports environment variables that can store values like API keys, endpoints, and authentication tokens, making it easier to manage different environments (e.g., development, staging, production).

Example of a collection for testing the **User Service**:

- o **GET /users**: Fetch a list of users.
- o **POST /users**: Create a new user.
- o **PUT /users/:id**: Update a user's information.
- o **DELETE /users/:id**: Delete a user.

2. **Writing and Running Tests in Postman**: Postman allows you to write tests directly in the app using JavaScript. For example, to check if the response status is 200 OK:

```javascript
pm.test("Response status is 200", function
() {
    pm.response.to.have.status(200);
```

```
});
```

3. **Automating Tests**: Postman supports running collections in **Newman** (Postman's command-line tool), which allows you to automate API tests. This can be useful for running end-to-end tests in a CI/CD pipeline.

   o   Install **Newman**:

   bash

   ```
   npm install -g newman
   ```

   o   Run a collection:

   bash

   ```
   newman run my-collection.json
   ```

4. **Continuous Integration with Postman**: You can integrate Postman tests with CI/CD tools like **Jenkins**, **GitLab CI**, or **CircleCI** to automate API testing in your development pipeline.

Simulating High Traffic and Load Testing

Load testing is essential to ensure that microservices can handle high traffic and scale effectively. By simulating real-world user behavior, you can identify bottlenecks and weaknesses in your services.

Tools for Load Testing:

1. **Apache JMeter**:
   - **JMeter** is a popular open-source tool for performance testing. It allows you to simulate a large number of users sending requests to your services and measure response times, throughput, and error rates.

2. **Artillery**:
   - **Artillery** is a modern, powerful, and easy-to-use tool for load testing microservices. It allows you to simulate high traffic, monitor performance, and generate detailed reports.

   Example of an Artillery script (`load-test.yml`):

```yaml
config:
  target: 'http://localhost:3000'
  phases:
    - duration: 60
      arrivalRate: 10
scenarios:
  - flow:
```

```
- get:
    url: '/users'
```

This script simulates 10 requests per second to the /users endpoint for 60 seconds.

3. **Gatling**:
   - **Gatling** is a load testing tool designed for high-performance tests. It can simulate large numbers of virtual users and generate detailed reports on response times, throughput, and performance.

4. **K6**:
   - **K6** is a developer-centric open-source load testing tool that is designed to be easy to use, fast, and scalable. It integrates well with modern CI/CD pipelines.

Real-World Example: Stress-testing a Product Catalog Microservice

Let's walk through an example of stress-testing a **Product Catalog Microservice** to ensure it can handle high traffic and perform well under load.

1. **Microservice Overview**:
   - The **Product Catalog Service** exposes an API that allows clients to retrieve product

information, add new products, update product details, and delete products.

o The endpoints might look like:

- GET /products: Retrieve all products.

- POST /products: Add a new product.

- PUT /products/:id: Update product details.

- DELETE /products/:id: Delete a product.

2. **Stress-testing with Artillery**:

o Create a script to simulate high traffic to the product catalog API.

Example of an Artillery script for testing the GET /products endpoint:

yaml

```yaml
config:
  target: 'http://localhost:3000'
  phases:
    - duration: 60
      arrivalRate: 50    # Simulate 50
requests per second
    - duration: 180
      arrivalRate: 100    # Simulate 100
requests per second
scenarios:
```

```
- flow:
    - get:
        url: '/products'
```

- o This script simulates 50 requests per second for the first 60 seconds and then increases to 100 requests per second for the next 180 seconds.
- o Run the test:

```bash
bash
```

```
artillery run load-test.yml
```

3. **Analyzing Results**: After running the test, analyze the results:

   - o **Response Times**: Look for any spikes in response times that could indicate bottlenecks.
   - o **Error Rates**: Ensure that error rates are low and that the system can handle the load without failing.
   - o **Throughput**: Measure how many requests per second the service can handle while maintaining acceptable response times.

4. **Identifying Bottlenecks**: If you notice performance degradation under load (e.g., high response times or increased error rates), you may need to:

- o **Optimize Database Queries**: Slow queries could be a bottleneck. Use indexing or caching to speed up database lookups.
- o **Horizontal Scaling**: Add more instances of the service to distribute the load.
- o **Improve Caching**: Cache frequently accessed data to reduce load on the backend.

Conclusion

In this chapter, we discussed the challenges and strategies for **testing microservices at scale**. We covered tools like **Postman** for end-to-end testing, as well as load testing tools like **Artillery**, **JMeter**, and **Gatling** to simulate high traffic and identify performance bottlenecks. We also provided a real-world example of **stress-testing** a **Product Catalog Microservice** to ensure it can handle high loads and maintain performance. By implementing effective testing practices, you can ensure that your microservices architecture is reliable, scalable, and resilient under real-world conditions.

CHAPTER 23

HANDLING TRANSACTIONS IN MICROSERVICES

In a microservices architecture, handling transactions can be complex due to the distributed nature of the services. Unlike monolithic systems, where transactions are typically handled by a single database, microservices often need to manage transactions that span multiple services and databases. Ensuring that these transactions are reliable and consistent across services is crucial for maintaining data integrity and system stability. In this chapter, we will explore the concept of **distributed transactions**, discuss patterns like **Saga** and **two-phase commit** for managing transactions, and look at **eventual consistency**. We will also provide a real-world example of **handling payment transactions** across services.

Introduction to Distributed Transactions

A **distributed transaction** is a transaction that involves multiple services or systems, each potentially managing its own database. In the context of microservices, each service is typically responsible for its own data store, and transactions often need to span across these services. This presents challenges in ensuring **data consistency** and **atomicity**—the two key properties of transactions.

In traditional monolithic applications, transactions are handled by a single relational database, and transactions are often ACID (Atomicity, Consistency, Isolation, Durability) compliant. However, in microservices architectures, we must handle transactions that span multiple services, each with its own database, and this makes the ACID properties difficult to achieve.

Distributed Transactions need to ensure:

- **Atomicity**: All parts of the transaction must succeed, or none should. If any part fails, the entire transaction should fail.
- **Consistency**: The system should be in a consistent state before and after the transaction.
- **Durability**: Once a transaction is committed, it should not be lost, even in the event of a system failure.

To handle distributed transactions, we need to use specialized patterns and techniques, which we will discuss in the next sections.

Using Saga and Two-Phase Commit for Transactions

There are several strategies for managing distributed transactions in microservices. Two of the most common patterns are **Saga** and **Two-Phase Commit (2PC)**.

1. Saga Pattern

The **Saga Pattern** is a sequence of local transactions where each service involved in the transaction performs a part of the overall transaction. If one of the services fails, compensating actions are taken to revert the changes made by the other services, ensuring eventual consistency across the system.

Sagas are typically implemented using two approaches:

- **Choreography**: In this approach, each service involved in the saga knows which other services to communicate with and how to trigger the next action in the saga. There is no central coordinator; instead, services publish events that other services listen for.
- **Orchestration**: In this approach, a central coordinator (a service or process) controls the entire saga by sending commands to each service and waiting for responses.

Advantages of Saga:

- **Scalability**: Since each service is responsible for its part of the transaction, the system can scale easily.
- **Resilience**: If one service fails, compensating actions can be taken, and the system can recover.
- **Decoupling**: Services are loosely coupled and interact asynchronously, making the system more flexible.

Disadvantages of Saga:

- **Complexity**: Implementing the saga pattern, especially with orchestration, can be complex and require careful error handling.
- **Eventual Consistency**: Sagas are based on eventual consistency, which means the system may not be fully consistent at all times.

Example of Saga: Consider a user placing an order:

1. The **Order Service** starts the transaction by creating an order.
2. The **Payment Service** charges the customer's card.
3. The **Inventory Service** updates the stock.
4. The **Shipping Service** schedules the delivery.

If the **Payment Service** fails, a compensating transaction is triggered to cancel the order creation and notify the user.

2. Two-Phase Commit (2PC)

The **Two-Phase Commit (2PC)** protocol is a traditional way of handling distributed transactions. In 2PC, a **coordinator** service manages the transaction and coordinates the participants (services).

How 2PC Works:

- **Phase 1 (Prepare)**: The coordinator asks each participant (service) whether they are ready to commit the transaction. Each participant performs its part of the transaction (e.g., reserving funds, updating stock) and sends a "prepare" message to the coordinator.
- **Phase 2 (Commit or Abort)**: If all participants respond with "yes," the coordinator sends a "commit" message, and all participants finalize the transaction. If any participant responds with "no," the coordinator sends an "abort" message, and all participants roll back their changes.

Advantages of 2PC:

- **Atomicity**: 2PC ensures that all participants either commit or abort the transaction, maintaining atomicity.
- **Consistency**: All services involved in the transaction are guaranteed to reach the same decision (commit or abort).

Disadvantages of 2PC:

- **Blocking**: If a participant or coordinator fails during the transaction, the system may get stuck in a blocked state until the failure is resolved.

- **Single Point of Failure**: The coordinator is a single point of failure. If the coordinator crashes, the entire system may be affected.

- **Performance**: 2PC can be slow due to the need for multiple network round trips between participants.

Managing Eventual Consistency in Microservices

Eventual consistency is a concept where the system guarantees that, given enough time, all services will reach a consistent state, but it does not guarantee consistency at any specific point in time. This is a common approach in microservices because distributed systems often involve delays and failures that make achieving strict consistency difficult.

Key strategies for managing eventual consistency in microservices include:

- **Event-Driven Architecture**: Services communicate asynchronously via events. For example, when an order is placed, an "OrderCreated" event is emitted. Other services (e.g., Payment Service, Inventory Service) subscribe to this event and take action when they receive it.

- **Compensating Transactions**: If a failure occurs, compensating transactions (or rollbacks) are used to undo actions taken by previous services. For example, if a payment fails after an order is created, a compensating transaction could cancel the order.

- **Retries and Idempotency**: Services can retry failed operations and handle them in an idempotent manner, meaning that if an operation is repeated, it has the same effect as performing it once.

Real-World Example: Handling Payment Transactions Across Services

Let's consider a scenario where a **Payment Transaction** involves multiple services in a microservices architecture. The services involved include:

1. **Order Service** (creates the order),
2. **Payment Service** (charges the user),
3. **Inventory Service** (updates product stock),
4. **Shipping Service** (prepares the shipment).

We will use the **Saga Pattern** to manage the transaction and ensure consistency across the services.

1. **Step 1: Order Service Creates the Order**: The **Order Service** starts the saga by creating the order in its database and emitting an `OrderCreated` event.

2. **Step 2: Payment Service Charges the User**: The **Payment Service** listens for the `OrderCreated` event, processes the payment, and emits an `PaymentProcessed` event.

   o If the payment fails, the **Payment Service** emits a `PaymentFailed` event, and the **Order Service** will trigger a compensating transaction to cancel the order.

3. **Step 3: Inventory Service Updates Stock**: The **Inventory Service** listens for the `PaymentProcessed` event and reduces the stock of the purchased items.

   o If stock is insufficient, the **Inventory Service** emits a `StockInsufficient` event, and the **Order Service** will cancel the order.

4. **Step 4: Shipping Service Prepares Shipment**: The **Shipping Service** listens for the `PaymentProcessed` event and schedules the shipment.

   o If shipping is delayed, the **Shipping Service** emits a `ShippingDelayed` event, and the **Order Service** will notify the customer.

5. **Step 5: Compensating Transactions**: If any service fails during the saga, compensating transactions are triggered to undo previous actions. For example, if the **Payment**

Service fails, the **Order Service** will cancel the order and notify the user.

Conclusion

In this chapter, we explored how to handle distributed transactions in microservices. We discussed the **Saga Pattern** and the **Two-Phase Commit (2PC)** protocol as two ways to manage transactions across services. We also looked at how **eventual consistency** can be achieved in microservices through techniques like event-driven architecture, compensating transactions, and retries. Finally, we provided a **real-world example** of how to handle **payment transactions** across services using the Saga Pattern to ensure consistency and resilience in a microservices-based system.

By implementing these transaction management strategies, you can ensure that your microservices architecture maintains data integrity, handles failures gracefully, and scales efficiently.

CHAPTER 24

BEST PRACTICES AND FUTURE OF NODE.JS MICROSERVICES

As microservices architectures become more popular, it's crucial to follow best practices to ensure that the system remains resilient, scalable, and easy to maintain. Additionally, when transitioning to microservices from legacy systems, careful planning and strategy are necessary. In this chapter, we'll explore **best practices** for building resilient microservices, discuss how to handle **legacy systems** while adopting microservices, and take a look at the **future of microservices in Node.js**. We will also provide a **real-world example** to reflect on the lessons learned from building and maintaining a large-scale microservice architecture.

Best Practices for Building Resilient Microservices

Building resilient microservices is critical to ensure that your system can handle failures and traffic spikes without compromising performance or availability. The following best practices can help make your microservices more resilient:

1. **Design for Failure**:

271

- Microservices are inherently distributed, which means failures are inevitable. You should design your services to be fault-tolerant, meaning they should continue functioning even when other services fail. Use techniques like **circuit breakers**, **retry mechanisms**, and **timeouts** to prevent cascading failures.

- **Example**: Implement a **circuit breaker** pattern to temporarily stop requests to a service if it is failing repeatedly, and then retry later.

2. **Use Idempotency**:

- Idempotency ensures that making the same request multiple times results in the same outcome. This is crucial in a distributed system where retries or duplicate requests may occur due to network failures.

- **Example**: For payment transactions, ensure that the same payment request cannot be processed more than once, even if it is retried.

3. **Service Autonomy**:

- Each microservice should be designed to be as autonomous as possible. It should handle its own data, own its lifecycle, and interact with other services through well-defined APIs.

- **Example**: A **User Service** should manage user data independently and communicate with other services like **Order Service** only when necessary.

4. **API Versioning**:
   o API versioning allows you to make changes to the service without breaking existing consumers. You can use strategies like **URI versioning** or **header versioning** to support backward compatibility.
   o **Example**: `/api/v1/users` for the first version and `/api/v2/users` for the next version, allowing clients to migrate at their own pace.

5. **Asynchronous Communication**:
   o Using asynchronous communication (e.g., **event-driven architecture** or **message queues**) reduces the coupling between services, allowing them to operate independently and handle failures more gracefully.
   o **Example**: An **Order Service** could emit an event (like `OrderCreated`) that the **Payment Service** listens for to process the payment asynchronously.

6. **Health Checks and Monitoring**:
   o Always expose health check endpoints to ensure that your microservices are running smoothly. Additionally, use monitoring tools like **Prometheus** and **Grafana** to monitor the health,

performance, and resource usage of your services in real time.

- o **Example**: A `/health` endpoint should check the status of your service and its dependencies (e.g., database, external APIs).

7. **Automated Testing and Continuous Integration**:
   - o Testing is essential to maintain the reliability of microservices. Implement unit, integration, and end-to-end tests. Also, set up **CI/CD** pipelines to automate testing, building, and deploying services.
   - o **Example**: Use tools like **Jenkins** or **GitHub Actions** for automated testing and deployment pipelines.

Handling Legacy Systems While Adopting Microservices

Transitioning from a monolithic architecture or legacy system to microservices is challenging, but with the right approach, it can be done smoothly. Here are some strategies for managing this transition:

1. **Strangling the Monolith**:
   - o The **Strangler Fig Pattern** is a strategy to gradually replace parts of a monolithic system with microservices. You begin by extracting one

piece of functionality (e.g., the user authentication module) from the monolith and refactoring it into a microservice, while the rest of the monolith remains in place.

o **Example**: Start with migrating the **order management** feature of the monolithic app into a separate microservice, and then gradually move other features to microservices.

2. **API Gateway for Interoperability**:

o Use an **API Gateway** to integrate legacy systems with your new microservices. The API Gateway can act as a middle layer, allowing both old and new systems to communicate with each other.

o **Example**: The **API Gateway** can route requests to either the monolithic system or the new microservice, depending on which functionality is being requested.

3. **Database Migration Strategy**:

o In microservices, each service usually has its own database. You'll need a strategy to migrate from a monolithic database to a decentralized database architecture. This can be done by gradually separating the database for each service while maintaining the monolith's database during the transition.

- o **Example**: Start by extracting the **user database** from the monolithic database and migrating it to a new database managed by the **User Service**. Keep the monolithic database intact while gradually migrating other parts of the database.

4. **Gradual Refactoring**:
   - o Instead of rewriting everything from scratch, you can refactor the monolithic codebase over time. Break down the monolith into smaller components and migrate them into microservices.
   - o **Example**: If you have an e-commerce platform, you could first refactor the product catalog feature into a microservice, and later move the checkout system, inventory management, and order processing into separate services.

The Future of Microservices in Node.js: Trends and Emerging Technologies

Microservices continue to evolve, and new trends and technologies are shaping the future of how microservices are built and maintained in Node.js. Here are some emerging trends:

1. **Serverless Architecture**:
   - o Serverless computing is gaining popularity, where cloud providers manage the infrastructure,

allowing developers to focus on writing code. Services like AWS Lambda, Azure Functions, and Google Cloud Functions allow you to run microservices without managing servers.

- o **Example**: You could use **AWS Lambda** to run small, stateless microservices that handle specific tasks like processing payment or sending email notifications.

2. **Event-Driven Microservices**:

- o Asynchronous communication and event-driven architectures are becoming the standard for microservices. Technologies like **Apache Kafka**, **RabbitMQ**, and **NATS** enable microservices to communicate through events, improving scalability and fault tolerance.

- o **Example**: A **Payment Service** could emit an event (`PaymentSuccessful`) that other services (like **Order Service** and **Inventory Service**) can listen to and react accordingly.

3. **Service Mesh**:

- o A **Service Mesh** is a dedicated infrastructure layer that handles service-to-service communication, monitoring, and security in microservices environments. Tools like **Istio** and **Linkerd** provide features like traffic management, security (mTLS), and observability (metrics and tracing) for microservices.

- o **Example**: A **Service Mesh** can handle retries, circuit breaking, and load balancing between microservices, enabling better fault tolerance.

4. **API-First Development**:

- o The **API-first** approach focuses on designing APIs before implementing the services. This ensures that APIs are standardized, versioned, and documented, making it easier for teams to develop services independently and interact seamlessly.

- o **Example**: Use tools like **Swagger** or **OpenAPI** to design and document the APIs first, and then generate client libraries or server stubs for the microservices.

5. **Microservices on Kubernetes**:

- o Kubernetes continues to be the go-to platform for orchestrating and managing microservices. Kubernetes provides features like automated scaling, load balancing, service discovery, and fault tolerance for running microservices in production.

- o **Example**: Kubernetes can automatically scale up your **Order Service** during high traffic periods and scale it down during periods of low demand, ensuring efficient resource usage.

6. **Machine Learning and AI Integration**:

   o   As microservices become more intelligent, there's a growing trend to integrate **Machine Learning (ML)** and **Artificial Intelligence (AI)** models into microservices. ML models can be deployed as microservices to handle tasks like fraud detection, recommendation systems, or predictive analytics.

   o   **Example**: An **AI-powered fraud detection service** could analyze transactions in real time and trigger alerts or block suspicious transactions.

Real-World Example: Lessons Learned from Building and Maintaining a Large-Scale Microservice Architecture

Let's reflect on the lessons learned from building and maintaining a large-scale microservices architecture for an **e-commerce platform**.

1. **Challenges**:

   o   **Managing Service Dependencies**: As the number of microservices grew, managing inter-service communication and dependencies became complex. We relied heavily on **API Gateways** to simplify interactions between services.

o **Data Consistency**: Maintaining data consistency across distributed services was a challenge. We implemented the **Saga Pattern** for transactions, ensuring that compensating actions were taken when a service failed.

2. **Solutions**:

o **Centralized Logging and Monitoring**: We used the **ELK Stack** (Elasticsearch, Logstash, and Kibana) and **Prometheus** with **Grafana** for centralized logging and monitoring. This allowed us to quickly identify performance bottlenecks and errors in the system.

o **Automated Testing**: We integrated **CI/CD pipelines** using **Jenkins** to automate testing, building, and deploying services. This helped ensure that updates were deployed quickly and reliably without affecting the overall system.

o **Scaling and Performance**: We used **Kubernetes** for container orchestration, allowing us to easily scale microservices up or down based on traffic demand. Additionally, **load testing** with tools like **Artillery** helped us ensure that the platform could handle high volumes of traffic during peak times.

3. **Key Takeaways**:

   o **Start small**: Begin by migrating smaller, less critical services to microservices before tackling the core functionality.

   o **Embrace event-driven architecture**: Event-driven communication between services reduces coupling and improves fault tolerance.

   o **Prioritize monitoring and observability**: With so many services, having a strong monitoring and logging system is essential for troubleshooting and performance optimization.

Conclusion

In this chapter, we discussed **best practices** for building resilient microservices, such as designing for failure, using idempotency, and managing service dependencies. We also explored how to handle **legacy systems** during the transition to microservices and looked at the **future of microservices in Node.js** with emerging technologies like **serverless, event-driven architectures**, and **service meshes**. Finally, we provided a **real-world example** of the lessons learned from building and maintaining a large-scale microservice architecture, emphasizing the importance of monitoring, testing, and scaling. By following these best practices and leveraging modern tools and patterns, you can build scalable, resilient, and maintainable microservices architectures.

www.ingramcontent.com/pod-product-compliance
Lightning Source LLC
LaVergne TN
LVHW052128070326
832902LV00039B/4088